JN057399

Comprehensive Strategies for English Listening

英語リスニング これ一冊

リスニング問題に強くなる徹底トレーニング

津村元司 著

執筆協力・英文校閲　Paul Aaloe

ベレ出版

はじめに

「シャドーイングを毎日やっているのに、TOEIC や英検のリスニング点数が伸びません。聞こえているのに、英語が頭からすぐに消えてしまうんです。」

これは、私のリスニングクラスに初めて参加した生徒さんたちからよく聞く言葉です。「英語が聞こえているのに、頭からすぐに消えてしまう。」という感覚を持っている人は多いのではないでしょうか。シャドーイングを頑張っているのにリスニング力が上がらないのはなぜでしょうか?

英語のリスニング本といえば「シャドーイング」という言葉をよく耳にします。しかし、一般の英語学習者、特に初級、中級の学習者がどれほどシャドーイングを理解しているのでしょうか。多くの人は、シャドーイングはテキストを見ずに音声に合わせて英語を声に出すことくらいしか理解していないように思えます。みなさんは、シャドーイングには2種類あるということを知っていますか?

2種類のシャドーイング

英語のリスニング力強化のためにおこなうシャドーイングは、プロソディー・シャドーイングとコンテンツ・シャドーイングの2種類があります。

プロソディー・シャドーイング (prosody shadowing)

prosody は日本語では「音韻」という意味で、プロソディー・シャドーイングは文字通り「音を真似る」シャドーイングです。これが一般的にシャドーイングとして多くの英語学習者がおこなっている方法です。意味に関係なく、ネイティブスピーカーの発音に合わせて、できるだけ音を真似る方法です。

コンテンツ・シャドーイング（contents shadowing）

プロソディー・シャドーイングのあとにコンテンツ・シャドーイングという練習をします。これは、英語の語順で英文の内容を理解する訓練です。プロソディー・シャドーイングとは違い、英語の語彙力や文法力も必要です。逆に言えば、この工程を経ることで、耳から英語の情報を正しく獲得できます。

シャドーイングのレベル

シャドーイングは元々同時通訳者がおこなう練習ですが、プロの通訳者のシャドーイング練習は「自分の英語力マイナス1」の英語マテリアルを使うと聞いたことがあります。英語の初級、中級者では初級の英会話レベルです。

聞こえたはずの英語がすぐに消える謎

最初に登場した生徒さんたちのように、シャドーイングをいくらやってもリスニング力が上がらないという方がよく来られます。今までの経験では、このようなパターンの方は、プロソディー・シャドーイングしかおこなっていないことがわかりました。それに加えて、実力マイナス1どころか実力プラス2や3の教材を使っているのです。頑張り屋さんほど高いレベルの教材を使う傾向があるようです。

それが、なぜ効果的な学習にならないのでしょうか？それは、英語の音を追うのに精一杯で、英語の語順で内容を聞き取り理解していく余力が残っていないのです。これは、歌詞の意味を理解しないで、洋楽を歌っている状態に近いと言えます。このために、「英語が聞こえているのに、すぐに消えてしまう」ということが起こるのです。

本書の特徴

本書では、プロソディー・シャドーイングで獲得する「英語らしい音に慣れる」練習と、コンテンツ・シャドーイングで獲得する「英語を聞きながら意味を理解する」練習を両方おこないます。しかし、この本はシャドーイングの本ではありません。段階ごとに、英語を見ながらおこなう練習と見ないでおこなう練習を合わせています。UNIT 1 から UNIT 3 の三部構成です。

UNIT 1 はプロソディーの練習です。最初からテキストを見ないで練習する必要はまったくありません。むしろ、見ながら自分が知っている英語と実際の発音の違いを、目と耳を使って合わせていく練習をしましょう。

UNIT 2 はコンテンツを聞き取る練習、つまり英語の語順に慣れて、長い文のコンテンツを日本語無しで理解する練習です。この練習はスピーキング力やリーディングでの速読力向上にも有効です。

UNIT 3 では英検や TOEIC のような試験形式の問題を使って、UNIT 1 とUNIT 2 で鍛えたリスニング力の力試しをします。なお問題は、英検、TOEIC などの資格試験を受けるためにリスニングを練習している人だけではなく、様々な目的でリスニング力をつけたい人を意識して作りました。したがって、英語圏の学校の講義やビジネスで使う、比較的フォーマルな英語だけでなく、海外で使える日常の口語表現も使っています。皆さんは英語の男性名 Joe が、口語で何を意味するか知っていますか?最近の若者のワーキング・スタイルを表す gig economy という表現がありますが、gig は聞いたことがありますか?答えは本書で探してください。

また、本書では UNIT 1 と UNIT 2 で練習した語やセンテンスが UNIT 3 の問題文にも使われています。UNIT 3 で UNIT 1、UNIT 2 の復習もできるように工夫されています。

以上が、本書の主な特徴です。十年以上、英語のリスニング力を伸ばすお手伝いをして、工夫してきたことを読者の皆さんにお伝えできるよう努力しました。

本書の英文校正は、前著「英語ライティングこれ一冊」と同様に関西学院大学非常勤講師の Paul Aaloe 先生にお願いしました。本書では、Paul 先生に執筆協力者として、UNIT 3 の問題作成にも関わっていただきました。Paul 先生の豊富な英語知識と、良い英語を読者に届けたいという真摯な姿勢にいつも助けていただいています。

読者目線で校正のお手伝いやアドバイスをいただいた吉川由恵さん、田中奈津子さんにもお礼申し上げます。

最後になりましたが、この本を書くきっかけをくださり、まとまりない文章を根気強く編集していただいたベレ出版編集部、大石裕子さんはじめベレ出版の皆様に感謝申し上げます。

本書が英語リスニング力を伸ばしたい読者の一助になれば無上の喜びです。

2021年4月

津村　元司

目次

音声ダウンロード方法

・付属音声をベレ出版ホームページより無料でダウンロードできます。
（MP3ファイル形式）

1. パソコンのウェブブラウザを立ち上げて「ベレ出版」ホームページ（www.
   beret.co.jp）にアクセスします。

2. 「ベレ出版」ホームページ内の検索欄から、『英語リスニングこれ一冊』の詳
   細ページへ。

3. 「音声ダウンロード」をクリック。

4. 8ケタのダウンロードコードを入力しダウンロードを開始します。
   ダウンロードコード：ztTYkLKK

5. パソコンやMP3音声対応のプレーヤーに転送して、再生します。

お願いと注意点について

・デジタルオーディオ、スマートフォンへの転送・再生方法など、詳しい操作方法に
ついては小社では対応しておりません。製品付属の取り扱い説明書、もしくは製造
元へお問い合わせください。

・音声は本書籍をお買い上げくださった方へのサービスとしてご提供させていただい
ております。様々な理由により、やむを得なくサービスを終了することがあります
ことをご了承ください。

UNIT 1

音声理解のリスニング
——英語の音に慣れる

▶英語の音と日本語の音の違い

この UNIT では英語独特の音のつながりに慣れる練習をします。日本語と英語の音のつながりの違いを見ましょう。先に日本語の例です。

　　　　日本語 = これは本（ほん）です。（koreha hon desu）

なにか気づきましたか？そうです。日本語はカナ文字ひとつひとつに母音（音節）があります。では英語はどうでしょうか？

英語の it を読んでみましょう。ittu（イットゥ）や itto（イット）と発音していませんか？ 日本語のように t に母音の u や o を足して読んでしまいますね。でも it は t に母音がないので「イッ」になり、what は wattu や watto ではなく wat（ワッ）です。例を出します。

英語 = What is it?
　　　英語の発音　　watizit　　母音（音節）3つ
　　　　　　　　　　<u>ワ ティ ジッ</u>
　　　　　　　　　　　1　2　3
　　　日本語式発音　　wattu izu ittu　　母音（音節）6つ
　　　　　　　　　　　<u>ワットゥ イ ズ イットゥ</u>
　　　　　　　　　　　1　　 2 3 4 5　6

例の What is it は音がつながって、発音される母音が3つですが、日本語の発音では母音が倍の6つになります。このような違いに慣れていない人は英語を聞いても、英語の音と自分が知っている英語表現を合わせることができずに混乱してしまいます。英語の音声の特徴を理解するために、英語の内用語と機能語についてお話ししましょう。

▶内容語 (content words) と機能語 (function words)

内容語 = 名詞、動詞、形容詞、副詞 など。文の主要な内容を表現する。
機能語 = 代名詞、助動詞、前置詞、接続詞、冠詞など。文法的機能で内
　　　　容表現を補助する。

例：Mr. Suzuki goes on a business trip to China.
　　　内　　　内　　機機　　内　　　内機　　内

You should give her a call soon.
　機　　　機　　　内　機　機内　内

内 = 内容語　　　機 = 機能語

英語の発音で省略されたり短くなるのは、主に機能語です。英語リスニングでは機能語の省略や音のつながりに慣れることが重要です。

▶UNIT 1の目標

英語らしい発音に慣れるために、目で確認しながら英語の音を聞き、口に出す練習をします。「勉強」というより「練習」です。Part 1 品詞別フレーズのリスニング、Part 2 センテンスのリスニングの二部構成です。まず、Part 1で英語の音に慣れましょう。英語の音に慣れてきたらPart 2で実践的なセンテンスリスニングの練習です。Part 1、Part 2とも最後に練習問題があります。

Part 1
品詞別フレーズのリスニング

代名詞、前置詞、助動詞など、品詞別に音のつながりや省略に注意して2〜3語の「語のかたまり」のリスニング練習をします。

▶ 練習の手順

音声は各語を3回繰り返します。
1. テキストを見ながら聞きます。特に太字部分の音に注意しましょう。
2. テキストを見ながら音に合わせて英語を発音します。
3. できるだけテキストを見ないで音について発音します。

この練習を繰り返して、テキストを見ないで英語を聞いて、英語の音声と頭に浮かぶ文字が一致すればオーケーです。

◁)) Track 01

1. 代名詞　it, he / his / him, her, us, you など

《I, our, us》

you and I　/　tell us　/　of us　/　get our permission
ユア**ナイ**　　**テ**ラス　　オ**バ**ス　　**ゲダ**ポミション

《you, your, yourself》

would you　/　ask yourself　/　need your help
ウヂュ　　　　　　アス**キヨ**セルフ　　　　ニー**ジョ**ヘルプ

《he, his, him》

when he　/　ask him　/　in his office
ウェ二　　　　アス**キム**　　　イ**ニゾ**フィス

《her, it, its》

in her office　/　repeat it　/　repeats it　/　repeated it
イ**ナ**オフィス　　リピー**ティッ**　　リピー**チッ**　　リピー**ティディッ**

2. 前置詞　in, on, at, about, of, above など

《in, on, of》

in an office　/　days in Osaka　/　clocks on the wall
イナノフィス　　　ディ**ジノ**サカ　　　　クロック**ソンザ**ウォール

a clock on the wall　/　hall of fame　/　of it　/　of her
アクロッ**コンザ**ウォール　　ホー**ロ**フェイム　　**オビッ**　　**オバ**

《at, about, above》

arrive at　/　talk about　/　above all
ァライ**バッ**　　トー**カ**バゥ　　ァバ**ボー**

arrived at / talked about / above yourself
ァライ**ヴダッ**　　　トーク**ダバゥ**　　　　ァバ**ビョ**セルフ

3. 熟語を作る in, on, along, up など

take in / take on / get along / bring up
テイ**キン**　　　テイ**コン**　　　　ゲ**ダ**ロン　　　ブリン**ガップ**

4. 助動詞と be 動詞

《be 動詞》

they **are** / there **are** / there **is** / **you are** / **he is**
　ゼ**ア**　　　　　　ゼ**ラ**　　　　　　ゼ**リズ**　　　　**ユァ＝ヨ**　　　**ヒズ**

they **aren't** / there **aren't** / there **isn't** / you **aren't** /
　ゼ**ア**(ン)　　　　　ゼ**ラ**(ン)　　　　　　ゼ**リズ**(ン)　　　　ユ**ア**(ン)

he **isn't**
ヒ**イズ**(ン)

◆ ワンポイントアドバイス
be 動詞は通常弱く発音するので聞こえにくく、特に are はほとんど聞こえな
いと思いましょう。否定の isn't や aren't の –'nt は弱いですが、-'nt を発音
するために is や are にアクセントが入って is や are は強く発音されます。つ
まり皆さんの耳で is や are がはっきり聞こえれば is や are ではなく、isn't や
aren't の可能性が高いのです。

《can と can't》

I **can** go / I **can't** go
アイ**クン**ゴゥ　アイ**キャン**ゴゥ

《should, would, could, might》

should **do** / would **go** / could **you** / might **eat**
シュッ**ドゥ**ー　　　　ウッ**ゴゥ**　　　　ク**ジュ**　　　　マイ**ディー**

《should have, would have, could have, might have》

shoul**d have** come / woul**d have** done / coul**d have** gone /
シュ**ダ**カム　　　　　　ウ**ダ**ダン　　　　　　　ク**ダ**ゴン

migh**t have** met
マイ**ダ**メッ

017

《完了形の have, has, had》

I'**ve been** / You'**d been** / She'**s gone** /
アイ**ビン**　　　　　ユッ**ビン**　　　　シ**ズゴン**

You and I **have been cheated**
ユアナイ**ァビンチーティッ**

練習問題

音声を聞いて空所に入る1～3語の英語をいれてください。1回聞いて答えを入れましょう。1問正解ごとに1点ですが、繰り返し聞くごとに0.2点引いてください。何回も聞けば得点がマイナスになります。

🔊 **Track 02**

1. Don' you think _____ time we upgraded our OS?

2. History _____ .

3. I _____ a package tour.

4. I told _____ BYOB.

5. A little girl has _____ mother.

6. Could _____ either by phone or e-mail?

7. I'd like to _____ these books.

8. I might _____ down.

9. I need to call _____ meeting with today.

10. I _____ for a while.

11. _____ a bunch of IT businesses using overseas call centers.

12. We should _____ a little further.

13. I _____ for the first time yesterday.

14. You've _____ with Daniel in R & D, right?

15. Fishery resources _____ depleted.

16. It looks like _____ next year's budget.

17. We will be _____ to _____ a bank loan.

18. _____ forced to take Route 1, because _____ bumper-to-bumper traffic on Green Drive.

19. He _____ the traditional Japanese inn.

20. I shouldn't begrudge _____ reward.

正解 _____ 問 － （聞き返し_____ 回 × 0.2） = _____ 点

満点　20点

解答

1. it's about　そろそろ私たちの OS をアップグレードする時期だと思わないかい？

2. repeats itself　歴史は繰り返す。

3. can get you　パッケージツアーをお取りできます。

4. them it's　お酒は持ち寄りだと言ってあるよ。
   ボキャブラリー　BYOB = Bring Your Own Booze（Bottle）お酒は各自持参

5. lost her　小さな女の子がお母さんとはぐれました。

6. you contact us　電話かメールでご連絡願えますか？

7. check out　これらの本を借り出したいんです。

8. have jotted it　それを書き留めたかもしれません。
   ボキャブラリー　jot down 書き留める

9. a client I'm　今日会う予定のクライアントに電話しないといけません。

10. haven't been here　しばらく来ていませんでした。

11. There're　海外のコールセンターを使っている IT 企業はたくさんあります。

12. look into it　もう少し詳しく調べてみるべきだ。

13. tried this on　私はこれを昨日初めて試着した。

14. been hanging around　研究開発部の Daniel とほっつき歩いてるん
でしょ？

ボキャブラリー　R & D = Research and Development 研究開発部

15. have been　漁業資源は（すでに）枯渇している。

ボキャブラリー　deplete 枯渇させる

16. it'll fit into　それは来年の予算に合致するように見える。

17. talking about how　take out
銀行ローンの引き出し方についてお話します。

18. They have been　there's been
彼らはルート1を使わざるを得なくなっている。なぜなら、Green Drive
はずっと大渋滞だから。

ボキャブラリー　bumper-to-bumper traffic 大渋滞

19. helps out at　彼は伝統的な（日本式）旅館を手伝う。

20. him his　彼の報酬を妬んだらだめだね。

ボキャブラリー　begrudge （人を）〜で妬む

Part 2
センテンスのリスニング

1. 短いセンテンスのリスニング

Part 1で練習した「語のかたまり」を短いセンテンスの中で聞きます。発音のカナカナ表記と日本語訳が付いています。この練習では、意味より音のつながりを意識しましょう。

▶ 練習の手順

音声は各センテンスを3回繰り返します。

1. ▮▮▮ 部分に注意して、テキストを見ながら聞きます。特に太字部分の音に注意しましょう。
2. ▮▮▮ 部分に注意して、テキストを見ながら音に合わせて英語を発音します。
3. テキストを見ないで聞いてみましょう。この時、音のつながりに意識して聞きます。

この練習を繰り返して、テキストを見ないで英語の音声と頭に浮かぶ文字が一致すればオーケーです。

◆重要

練習の手順3の段階で重要なことはシャドーイングのように、リスニングしながら英語を発音しません。耳に神経が集中できなくなります。耳に入ってくる音と自分が知っている英語が合致することが大事です。聞くだけではなく英文を発音することも大切ですが、音を確認する最終段階では耳に神経を集中してリスニング力が上がっていることを確認します。

ソウル**ダ**ゥ**ドビ**ッ
1. The shop sold out of it.
　そのお店はそれを売り切った。

アス**キョ**セルフ イ**フィティ**ズ
2. Ask yourself if it is right.
　それが正しいか自問しなさい。

ゼ**ア**　　　ァライ**キン**
3. They are so alike in character.
　彼らはすごく性格が似ている。

ヒヨァ　　　ジ**シジョ**ァズ
4. Here you are. This is yours.
　どうぞ。これはあなたのものです。

スタ**ディ**ングリッシュ
5. Many study English.
　多くの人が英語を勉強する。

トゥッ**カク**ション アヘ**ドヴ**
6. They took action ahead of time.
　彼らは先んじて行動を起こした。

バッ**キナナ**ワー
7. We'll be back in an hour.
　1時間で帰ってきます。

8. She **got across** the river.
ゴダクロス

彼女は川を渡った。

9. They **are in her** office.
_ゼ(ァ) イナ_

彼らは彼女のオフィスにいる。

10. They **were in his o**ffice.
_ゼワ イニゾ_フィス

彼らは彼のオフィスにいた。

🔊 **Track 04**

11. I **bought** this blouse here.
_ボ_

私はこのブラウスをここで買いました。

12. We are in the same **boat**.
_ボウ_

私たちは同じ境遇にある。

ボキャブラリー be in the same boat 同じ境遇にある。

13. We finally **caugh**t him **in his hideout**.
_コ_ティム _イニザイダウ_

我々は彼の隠れ家でようやく彼を捕まえた。

ボキャブラリー hideout 隠れ家

14. Camel is the most popular **coa**t color.
_コウ_

キャメル（黄褐色）はコートの色では一番人気がある。

ヒズ**ゲッディンガバ**ヴィムセルフ

15. He's **getting above him**self.

彼はうぬぼれ始めている。

ボキャブラリー　get above oneself　うぬぼれる

ユク**ニーディドー**

16. You **can eat it all**.

それを全部食べてもいいですよ。

ユ**キャン イーディドー**

17. You **can't eat it all**.

それを全部食べてはだめです。

アイ**ビニンタ**レス**ティディン**

18. I've been interested in world history.

私はずっと世界史に興味があります。

アイッ**ビナウェロビ**ズ

19. I'd been aware of his dishonesty.

彼の不誠実さはずっと気づいていた。

ク**ダダ**ニッ

20. You coul**d have done it** better.

もう少しうまくできただろうに。

＊結果が十分でなかった時にかける言葉。

クドゥンタダニッ
21. You coul**dn't have done it** better.
よくできました。（それ以上うまくできることはなかっただろう。）
＊何かがうまくできた時の褒め言葉。

ワッ**ヴュビナップ**トゥ
22. Wha**t've you been up** to lately?
最近どうしてたの？

ボキャブラリー　What have you been up to? 挨拶の言葉

スィンキ　ディ**ダナ**メイジン
23. I thin**k he** di**d an a**mazing job.
彼はすごいことをしたと思うよ。

スィン**キル**
24. I thin**k he'll** be a life saver.
彼が救い主になると思う。

ボキャブラリー　life saver 救い主、苦境を助けてくれる人

メイ**ディッ**
25. His efforts ma**de it** possible.
彼の努力がそれを可能にした。

ウッ　ファイン**ダウ**
26. Jenifer woul**d find out** the truth.
Jenifer は真実を発見するかもしれない。

27. Could **you** ask **him** to **call** her?
クヂュ アス**キム** コ**ラ**

彼女に電話するよう彼に頼んでくれますか？

28. You **should** come here **with** her.
シュッ ウィ**ザ**

あなたは彼女とここに来るべきだ。

29. You **should have** come here **with him**.
シュ**ダ** **ウィジム**

あなたは彼と来るべきだった。

30. James **spread out his** notes on the table.
スプレ**ダウティズ**

James は彼のメモをテーブルの上に広げた。

🔊 **Track 06**

31. Many **studied English** at **educ**ational institutions.
スタ**ディ**ディングリッシュ **アデジュ**ケイショナ

多くの人が教育機関で英語を勉強した。

32. Many **have** spoken **out on** various issues.
ア スポウク**ナウトン**

多くの人が様々な問題に声を上げてきた。

33. There**'re** other reasons **why it** happened.
ゼ**ラ** ワ**イッ**

それが起こった別の理由がある。

34. The protester would **have** expressed **her** opinion.

ウ**ダ**　　　イクスプレス**ダ**

その抗議者は自分の意見を発表しただろう。

35. She **gets** thrilled by **amu**sement park rides.

ゲッ**ツ**スリルドゥ　　**ミュー**ズメン

彼女は遊園地の乗り物にわくわくする。

◆ワンポイントアドバイス

amusement の a のように母音で始まる語で、その母音にアクセントが無ければほとんど聞こえません。日本語の「メリケンパーク」、「メリケンサック」などの「メリケン」は "American" の A が弱いので、日本人にはそのように聞こえるところから来ています。

---

36. He himself **was an au**thor **of** several books based on his life story.

ウォ**ザ**ノー**サ ロヴ**

彼自身が何冊かの自伝的な本の著者であった。

37. He's thin**king about** working **for an in**ternational corporation.

スィン**キナバ**　　　　フォ**ラニン**ターナショナ

彼は国際企業で働こうと考えている。

38. **This species** almost beca**me extinct in** the 20th century.

ズィ**スピー**シーズ　　　ビケイ**ミクス**ティンクティン

この種は20世紀にほとんど絶滅しかけた。

ボキャブラリー　species 種　extinct 絶滅した

アイドゥベタゴァヘッ

39. I'd better go ahead with my scheduled presentation.

予定が決まっているプレゼンを進めるべきだよね。

◆ **ワンポイントアドバイス**

I'd better ～「(自分が) ～すべきですね」はよく使いますが、you'd better ～
は命令調になるので注意が必要です。友達に助言する時は　You should ～が
よいでしょう。

　　I'd better go now.（そろそろ行かないといけません。）

　　You should go now.（そろそろ行った方がいいよ。）

ザダイワゾネッジ

40. I'm sorry that I was on edge.

イライラしてすみません。

ボキャブラリー　　on edge　イライラする

練習問題

音声を聞いて空所に入る英語を答えてください。語数指定はありません。まず、音声を1回だけ聞いて答えを入れましょう。1問正解ごとに1点ですが、繰り返し聞くごとに0.2点引いてください。何回も聞けば得点がマイナスになります。ヒントはできるだけ見ないで答えを出しましょう。

1. _____ all morning long.

2. In most cases, _____ bulk.
   > **ヒント** supply 資材、備品　in bulk 大量に

3. _____ him a job.

4. _____ name.
   > **ヒント** too ～ to ....するには～過ぎる。

5. _____ way home?
   > **ヒント** pick up（途中、途上で）買う

6. _____ lately?

7. _____ in1818 in Maryland.

8. _____ doctoral studies.

9. _____ .

10. _____ for millennia.

    ヒント be extinct 絶滅する　millennia millennium（千年）の複数形

11. _____ in the field.

    ヒント 分詞 done が名詞を後ろから修飾。

12. _____, if he'd asked us to.

13. _____, if he asked us to.

14. _____ on the rare occasion.

15. She sometimes has to leave work early

    _____.

16. _____.

17. _____.

18. _____ the managerial position for

our technical support team.

    ヒント 前置詞に続く動詞は動名詞。過去分詞 been は来ない。

19. _____ between us.

20. _____ to go camping.

正解 _____ 問 － （聞き返し_____ 回 × 0.2） = _____ 点

満点　**20**点

解答

1. You've been at your desk　午前中ずっと机に座りっぱなしですね。

2. building supplies are bought in
   たいてい、建築資材は大量購入される。

3. She's thinking of offering
   彼女は彼に仕事をオファーしようと思っている。

4. She's been too shy to give her
   彼女は恥ずかしくて名前が言えません。

5. Can you pick up some eggs on your
   帰りに卵を買ってきてくれる？

6. What've you been up to　最近どうしたの？

7. He was born a slave
   彼は1818年 Maryland で奴隷として生まれた。

8. He flies to London for his
   彼は博士号の勉強のため London に飛ぶ。＊fly ではない。

9. She returned to work　彼女は仕事に復帰した。
   ＊return、returns ではない。

10. Those species have been extinct
    これらの種は数千年間絶滅している。（数千年前に絶滅した。）

11. We were amazed at the research done
   私たちはその分野でなされた研究に驚いた。

12. We would have helped him
   もし彼が頼んでいたら私たちは彼を助けただろう。

13. We would help him　彼が頼むなら私たちは彼を助けるのですが。

14. We were thrilled　私たちはそのめずらしい機会にワクワクした。

15. because her son often has a fever
   彼女は息子が時々熱を出すので仕事を早く終えないといけない。

16. They caught some boats
   彼らは（何隻かの）ボートを捕まえた。

17. She bought a red coat　彼女は赤いコートを買った。

18. Thank you for being interested in　我が社の技術サポートチーム
   の管理職に興味を持っていただきありがとうございます。

   ◆ ワンポイントアドバイス
   動名詞、現在分詞 being と過去分詞 been を音で聞き分けるのは簡単で
   はないので、正確なリスニングのためには基本文法の知識も必要です。
   前置詞 for に続くのは分詞の been ではなく動名詞 being です。

19. There's been a problem　私たちの間にはずっと問題があります。

20. The children must have been thrilled
   子供たちはキャンプに行くことにワクワクしたに違いない。

2. 長いセンテンスのリスニング

長いセンテンスのリスニングでは、発音のカタカナ表記はありませんが、意味単位別にスラッシュ（/）で区切られています。音声を聞きながら文の区切り、文構造を理解する基本練習です。スラッシュ単位の細かい意味を意識せずに文の構造を理解します。例を出します。

例1：I will speak / on holding a successful meeting.
　　　主語＋動詞　　　前置詞＋名詞　（何について）

例2：As you know, / the demand for fish and other seafood /
　　　熟語　　　　　　　　　長い主語

is skyrocketing.

▶ 練習の手順

音声は各センテンスを3回繰り返します。

1. まずスラッシュを目安にして音声を区切って聞きます。
2. スラッシュの区切り単位で音声に合わせて読みます。ここまでは音声のつながりだけを意識します。
3. センテンスの最初から最後まで止めずに聞きます。音声のつながりと意味区切りを意識します。
4. センテンスの最初から最後までテキストを見ながら音声に合わせて読みます。
5. テキストを見ずに音声を聞いて音のつながりや省略、意味区切りの場所が理解できればオーケーです。

🔊 **Track 08**

1. Jasper blames all his business problems / on his colleagues / and stabs them in the back.

   Jasper は自分のビジネス上の問題で同僚たちを非難し、彼らを中傷する。

   （ボキャブラリー）　blame ～ on ... ～で…を非難する、stab in the back 陰口をたたく、中傷する

2. Something important would have gone wrong / if he hadn't done his best.

   彼がベストを尽くしていなかったら、何か重要なことがうまくいかなかっただろう。

3. Jasmine skipped out on her husband / after he'd quit his job / for the third time in a year.

   Jasmine は夫が一年で3回仕事を辞めた後、彼を置いて出て行った。

   （ボキャブラリー）　skip out on ～ ～を置いて出ていく

4. Because of the worsening economy, / more young guys picked up food delivery / as a side gig.

   経済がますます悪くなったので、食べ物の配達を副業にする若者が増えた。

   （ボキャブラリー）　side gig〈米口語〉（一時的な）副業

5. The task our team is being engaged in / is more demanding / than we thought it would be.

   我々のチームが従事している仕事は思っていたより骨が折れる。

   （ボキャブラリー）　demanding（仕事などが）手のかかる、きつい

6. The honoree arrived at the reception / and slowly realized / that all her friends and family were there.

その受賞者はレセプションに到着して、彼女の友達と家族が全員来ていることに徐々に気づいた。

ボキャブラリー honoree 受賞者

7. We conducted a survey / about consumer preferences of canned seafood / last month.

我々は先月、消費者の缶入りシーフードの好みに対する調査をおこなった。

8. The main building dates back to 1921 / but was well ahead of its time.

本館は1921年までさかのぼるが、その時代のかなり先を行っていた。

ボキャブラリー ahead of one's time 時代の先を行く

9. The students had been under the impression / that they couldn't get wireless in their classrooms / until their teachers promised them to.

学生たちは、先生が約束するまでは、教室がワイヤレスにならないという印象を持っていた。

10. The man is so much more independent / than when he left home.

その男性は家を出た時よりかなり自立している。

🔊 **Track 09**

11. Besides learning Chinese, / it was fun / meeting classmates from all over the world.

中国語を学ぶ以外に、世界中から来たクラスメイトに会うのが楽しかった。

12. We sat down and ordered / and couldn't eat it all / as we were all small eaters.

私たちは席に着いてオーダーした。そして、全員が少食だったので全部食べきれなかった。

13. Paying it off / in part or in full / at an early date / would indeed save you.

一部でも全額でも早いうちに支払い終えることは本当に助けになるかもしれない。

ボキャブラリー　pay off 支払い終える

14. You could end up depending on your kids / instead of supporting yourself after retirement.

退職後、最終的には自活できずに子供に頼らなければならなくなるかもしれない。

ボキャブラリー　end up 〜ing 最終的に〜することになる。

15. You could have had a great relationship / with your boss / in the beginning.

最初は上司と良い関係を持てていたかもしれない。

16. We all know what happens / when we have a ton of time / to do something; / we never get it done!

何かをする時間が十分あればどうなるかみんな知っている。何もしない！

17. Many are scared / that there are likely many jobs / that would be replaced by AI in the near future.

近い将来 AI に取って代わられる職業がたくさんあるかもしれないことを多くの人が恐れている。

ボキャブラリー　likely = probable 十分ありそうな、probably おそらく

18. There will likely be a lot of unintended consequences / of self-driving cars / that we have yet to imagine.

自動運転車に関して、私たちが考えたことがないような、意図しない結果になる可能性が大いにある。

19. According to a survey we conducted last month, / a fair percentage of the respondents feel / their Monday morning meetings are an annoyance.

私たちが先月おこなった調査によると、多くの割合の回答者が月曜の朝の会議がわずらわしいと感じている。

20. I hope / you've all had a chance / to look at the bar chart our department has handed out.

我が部が配布した棒グラフを見ていただいたと思います。

ボキャブラリー bar chart 棒グラフ

練習問題

音声を聞いて空所に入る英語を答えてください。長いセンテンスなので<u>語数</u>と<u>日本語訳</u>を提示します。主語や動詞などの文構造を意識しましょう。問題は15問で、1問1点で15点満点です。できるだけ少ない回数を聞いて答えを出しましょう。3回以上聞いた問題は正解しても0.5点引いてください。ヒントはできるだけ見ないで解答しましょう。

◆注意

日本語訳は直訳ではないので、英文と単語単位で一致しているとは限りません。省略形を含む語は1 word で数えます。つまり、We have や are not は2 words、We've や aren't は1 word です。

---

1. _____. (8 words)

Elegant エアライン101便ロンドン行きにご搭乗いただきありがとうございます。

ヒント　aboard 乗船して、搭乗して

2. _____. (7 words)

このシャツには悪いところはありません。

3. _____

_____. (11 words)

最近、私たちの電話サポートにたくさんのクレームが来ています。

ヒント　quite a few たくさんの　complaint 苦情、クレーム

4. _____. (10 words)

その新しい技術はなんらかの経済的利益をもたらす可能性がある。

5. Copernican theory _____

_____. (11 words)

地動説は地球やその他の惑星が太陽の周りを回っているということだ。

ヒント Copernican theory 地動説 revolve 回転する、自転する

6. The hurdy-gurdy _____

_____. (8 words)

ハーディー・ガーディーはヨーロッパ発祥の弦楽器だ。

ヒント stringed 弦の

7. Philadelphia _____

in the United States. (11 words)

Philadelphia はアメリカでもっとも通勤時間がかかる都市のひとつだ。

8. _____ cuppa joe.

(9 words)

何もやらずにコーヒーだけ飲んでいるみたいね。

ヒント cuppa cup of の口語表現 joe（米口語）コーヒー

9. _____, but if we don't get an upgrade,

_____ the competition. (6 words), (5words)

それでどうにかやっていけるけど、アップグレードしなければライバル
より優位に立てない。

ヒント get by on 〜 〜でどうにかやっていく、切り抜ける lose an edge
over 〜 〜に対して優位性を失う the competition（集合的に）競争
相手

10. _____ customers' heads.（9 words）

顧客が何を欲しているかを知るベストな方法を見つけなさい。

ヒント　get into one's head（人を）十分理解する

11. _____ checkup.（9 words）

あなたのカルテを見ると、健康診断で来られたんですね。

ヒント　chart（病院の）カルテ　checkup 健康診断

12. _____. （11 words）

家を買って資産形成するほうがよいかもしれないですよ。

ヒント　build up equity 資産形成する、 might prefer to 〜 〜する方がよい
でしょう。

13. _____. （12 words）

新しい技術を獲得するにはたくさんの時間と努力が必要だ。

ヒント　elbow grease たいへんな努力

14. The company _____ for the next fiscal
year.（8 words）

その会社は次の会計年度の総予算を削減すべきだった。

ヒント　fiscal year 会計年度（日本は4月1日から翌年3月31日）

15. _____. （7 words）

警察は未成年飲酒を取り締まる。

ヒント　crack down on 〜 〜を取り締まる

正解 _____ 問 － （3回以上聞き返し_____ 回 × 0.5) = _____ 点

満点　15点

解答

1. Welcome aboard Elegant Airline Flight 101 for London

2. There is nothing wrong with this shirt

3. We've recently had quite a few complaints about our telephone support

4. The new technology can bring with it some economic benefits

5. is that the earth and other planets revolve around the Sun

6. is a stringed musical instrument that originated in Europe

7. is one of the cities that has the longest commuting times

8. It looks like you've done nothing but sipping your

9. We can get by on it、 we'll lose an edge over

10. Find out the best way to get into our

11. Your chart says that you are here for your

12. You might prefer to buy a house and build up equity

13. Acquiring a new skill requires a lot of time and elbow grease

14. should have cut down on their total budget

15. The police crack down on underage drinking

UNIT 2

内容理解のリスニング
──英語の語順に慣れる

▶英語の語順

UNIT 2では英語の語順に慣れてリスニングの内容を理解する練習をします。UNIT 1で扱った英語独自の音声以外にも、英語の語順がリスニングの内容理解を難しくします。日本語と英語の語順を確認しましょう。 次の日本語を5秒で英語にしてください。

　　「わたしが買った本」

できましたか？ 　日本語が「わたし」で始まっているので、Iが最初に思い浮かびませんでしたか？ 　初級のリスニングクラスでこの質問をすると、多くの生徒さんが、「I bought …」と言いかけて止まってしまいます。"I bought a book." では「私は本を買った」になってしまいます。

　　日本語の語順　＝　<u>私が</u>　<u>買った</u>　<u>本</u>
　　　　　　　　　　　 I　　bought　a book

英語は後ろから説明する語順なので、「私が買った」は「本」の後ろに来ます。

　　英語の語順　＝　<u>a book</u>　<u>I bought</u>
　　　　　　　　　　　 本　　　私が買った

▶英語の5文型と修飾語

先の "I bought a book." は「私は本を買った」というセンテンスですが、語順通りに訳せば、「私は / 買った / 本を」です。語順が違うので英語を瞬時に日本語で理解することが難しいですね。3語ならどうにか理解できても、センテンスが長くなれば混乱します。リスニングの素早い内容理解のためには文構造を理解する必要があります。中学英語の復習を兼ねて英語の5文型を見ましょう。

1. S V (主語＋動詞)

That custom survived.
 S   V

その習慣は / 残った

2. S V C (主語＋動詞＋補語)

She got tired.
 S   V   C

彼女は / なった / 疲れた状態に

3. S V O (主語＋動詞＋目的語)

He needs help.
 S   V   O

彼は / 必要だ / 助けが

4. S V O O (主語＋動詞＋目的語1＋目的語2)

We offered her an opportunity.
 S   V O_1 O_2

我々は / 提供した / 彼女に / 機会を

5. S V O C (主語＋動詞＋目的語＋補語)

I made her happy.
 S   V   O   C

私は / した / 彼女を / 幸せに

この5文型の基本形に、場所、時間など、様々な情報（修飾語）が足されます。例を出します。SVO の文です。

例： 基本形
I got a position.
私は / 得た / 職を
↓

基本形 + 修飾語
I got a position at a trading company last month.
私は / 得た / 職を / 貿易会社で / 先月

例文の基本形は3語です。音声に慣れれば内容理解はそれほど難しくありません。修飾語が足されて語数が増えてくると混乱するのです。しかし、修飾語の種類の理解が素早い内容理解に役立ちます。もう一度例を見ましょう。

I got a position ＿＿＿＿＿＿＿＿ ＿＿＿＿＿＿＿ .

下線部に入る語を覚えていますか？漠然と英文を聞くより情報の種類を意識するだけで内容理解が容易になります。

I got a position 場所 時間 .

場所は「貿易会社」at a trading company、時間は「先月」last month でしたね。

▶UNIT 2の目標

UNIT 2では日本語とは違った英語の語順に慣れることでリスニングの内容を正確に理解する力を養います。この UNIT の日本語訳は英語の語順で示すので英語の語順で理解するようにしましょう。Part ごとに練習問題があるので練習の成果をチェックしましょう。

Part 1
後ろから説明を足す英語のリスニング

Part 1の構成

この Part には〈1. センテンスの修飾〉と〈2. 名詞の修飾〉があります。〈1. センテンスの修飾〉の修飾語には場所、時間などの情報、〈2. 名詞の修飾〉には英語の語順での日本語訳が示されています。 基本形 と 基本形＋修飾語 で一組になっています。

---

1. センテンスの修飾

1. 基本形

I'll meet with a client.
私は / 会う / クライアントに

↓

基本形＋修飾語

I'll meet with a client in Kyoto tomorrow.
                                   場所   時間

---

2. 名詞の修飾

1. 基本形

The man visited an old temple.
その男性は / 訪ねた / 古いお寺を

↓

基本形＋修飾語

The man studying the Japanese literature visited
その男性は / 研究している / 日本文学を

an old temple in Kyoto.
古いお寺を / 京都の

▶ 練習の手順

音声は各センテンスを3回繰り返します。

まず、基本形（各ペアの短い方）の練習をします。英文の下に英語の語順で日本語訳があります。

1. 英語を見て音声を聞きます。この時、日本語訳を参考にして英語の語順で英文を理解します。

2. 英文を見て音声に合わせて発音します。日本語は見ません。

3. 英文を見ないで音声を聞いた後に、語順を意識して英文を言います。

Ms. Lee	attended	a meeting.
誰が・何が	する・した	誰を・何を

基本形 の練習に続いて 基本形＋修飾語 （各ペアの長い方）の練習をします。

〈1. センテンスの修飾〉は場所、時間など、情報の種類を意識して練習します。〈2. 名詞の修飾〉は修飾語の語順を意識して練習します。詳しくは〈1. センテンスの修飾〉、〈2. 名詞の修飾〉の中でそれぞれ説明します。

1. センテンスの修飾のリスニング

「練習の手順」の説明に沿って 基本形 の練習をします。 基本形 の練習に続いて 基本形 + 修飾語 の練習をします。

基本形

Norman studied Japanese.
Norman は / 勉強した / 日本語を

↓

基本形 + 修飾語

Norman studied Japanese <u>in Australia</u> <u>for five years</u>.
　　　　　　　　　　　　　　　　場所　　　　　　　時間

基本形 + 修飾語 には日本語訳はありませんが、時間や場所など修飾語の種類が示されています。

▶練習の手順

音声は各センテンスを3回くり返します。

1. 英文を見て音声を聞きます。場所、時間、情報の種類や語順を意識します。
2. 英文を見ながら音声に合わせて発音します。情報の種類や英語の語順を意識します。
3. 英文を見ないで音声を聞いて、語順を意識して英文を言います。

この練習を繰り返して、文構造に沿って内容理解する力を養いましょう。

1. I want to go to the event.

   私は / 行きたい / イベントに

   I want to go to the event **at Pington Park** **on Saturday**.

   | 場所 | 時間 |

2. Daniel hurt his arm.

   ダニエルは / ケガをした / 腕を

   Daniel hurt his arm **during his PE class** **two days ago**.

   | 時間（場所） | 時間 |

   ボキャブラリー　PE class 体育の授業

3. Can you buy milk?

   あなたはできる？ / 買うことが / 牛乳を

   Can you buy milk **at the supermarket** **on your way home**?

   | 場所 | 時間（場所） |

4. James traveled.

   ジェームスは / 旅をした。

   James traveled **across ten countries** **for a year**.

   | 場所 | 期間 |

5. She will be going to their town.

   彼女は / 行くだろう / 彼らの町に

   She will be going to their town **next month** **on business**.

   | 時間 | 目的 |

6. I want to go to Canada.

私は / したい / 行くことを / カナダに

I want to go to Canada **someday to study English and their culture**.
　　　　　　　　　　　　　　　 時間　　　　　　　　　目的

ボキャブラリー　someday（未来の）いつか

7. Can I come?

できる？ / 私は / 行くことが

Can I come **to your house after school to study for the exam**?
　　　　　　　 場所　　　　　時間　　　　　　目的

8. I heard good things.

私は / 聞いた / 良いことを

I heard good things **about your school yesterday**.
　　　　　　　　　　　　 話題　　　　　　時間

053

9. Can I go ?

していい？ / 私は / 行くことを

Can I go **to the mall downtown with Mary tomorrow**?
　　　　　　 場所　　　　場所　　人（誰と）　　時間

10. Would you come?

しますか？ / あなたは / 来ることを

Would you come **with me to Mellisa Corporation**?
　　　　　　　　 人（誰と）　　　　　　場所

11. I need to speak.

   私は / 必要だ / 話すことが

   I need to speak **with my father about my plan after graduation**.

   人（誰と）　　　　　　話題（何について）

12. Our policy will change.

   我々の政策は / だろう / 変化する

   Our policy will change **with time and experience**.

   状況（何と共に）

13. The country caught up.

   その国は / 追いついた

   The country caught up **with the major industrialized countries in technology**.

   相手

   分野

14. We will be able to make a trip.

   我々は / できるだろう / 旅することを

   We will be able to make a trip **to Mars in the coming century**.

   場所　　　　時間

15. I would often talk.

   私は / よくしていた / 話すことを

   I would often talk **with him on the phone about everyday things**.

   人（誰と）　手段、道具　　話題

16. The rate is about 102 yen.

レートは / です / 約102円

The rate is about 102 yen **to the American dollar now**.

対象	時間

17. I had to go over.

私は / しなければならなかった / 行くことを

I had to go over **to the church for the christening today**.

場所	目的	時間

ボキャブラリー christening（キリスト教の）洗礼（式）、命名式

18. I can get a good deal.

私は / 得られる / 良い取引を

I can get a good deal **on flights and hotels**.

対象

ボキャブラリー deal 取引き

19. Dr. Smith speaks.

Smith 教授は / 話す

Dr. Smith speaks **on religion a couple of times a week**.

話題	回数	頻度

20. We calmly talked.

我々は / 静かに / 話した

We calmly talked **on the way to the house**.

時間（場所）	場所

21. The weather observatory has been shut down.

    気象観測所は / ままだ / 閉ざされた（状態）

    The weather observatory has been shut down **due to the blizzard**.　理由

    ボキャブラリー　observatory 観測所　blizzard 猛吹雪、暴風雪

22. His remarks made her change her mind.

    彼の発言は / した / 彼女を / 変えるように / 彼女の考えを

    His remarks made her change her mind **three times in a short period**.　回数　期間

23. She's arrived safely.

    彼女は到着した / 無事に

    She's arrived safely **at her mother's place after traveling by bike**.　場所　時間

24. Stacy makes it a rule to go for a walk.

    Stacy は / している / それを / ルールに /（それとは）散歩すること

    Stacy makes it a rule to go for a walk **in the park every day to stay fit**.　場所　頻度　目的

    ボキャブラリー　make it a rule to ～（必ず）～することにしている　stay fit 健康（な状態）を保つ

25. Taro and his sister leave home.

    太郎と妹は / 出る / 家を

    Taro and his sister leave home **for school at seven except for Sundays**.　場所（向けて）　時間　除外（…を除いて）

26. Bob answered the phone.

Bob は / 出た / 電話に

Bob answered the phone **for Mr. Douglas** **on the third ring** **during the meeting**. 代理 回数

期間

ボキャブラリー ring（電話の）呼び出し音

27. Bob got an e-mail.

Bob は / 受け取った / メールを

Bob got an e-mail **from Mr. Douglas** **within two days of his promotion**. 送り主 期間

28. We must offer the client a plan.

我々は / オファーしなければならない / クライアントに / プランを

We must offer the client a plan **by the end of this month to meet their demands**. 期限

目的

ボキャブラリー meet one's demand 要求に応える

057

29. The reporter read an article.

その記者は / 読んだ / 記事を

The reporter read an article **about corrupt politicians during the commute**. 話題 時間

ボキャブラリー corrupt politician 汚職の政治家 = 政治家の汚職

30. Mr. Yamaguchi was sick.

山口さんは / だった / 気分がすぐれない（状態）

Mr. Yamaguchi was **too** sick **to go to work** **right after the long voyage**. 度合（どれくらい） 時間

31. You should give her a ring.

あなたは / あげるべきだ / 彼女に / 電話を

You should give her a ring **first thing after lunch**.

順序　　　　　時間

32. She would get the okay and call me.

彼女は / 得るだろう / オーケーを / そして / 電話するだろう / 私に

She would get the okay **from her superiors** and call me **in the morning**.

人（誰から）

時間

33. They weren't honest.

彼らは / でなかった / 正直な（状態）

They weren't honest **with her about the root cause of their trouble**.

相手　　　　　　　　対象

ボキャブラリー　root cause　根本原因

34. I can't get my card reissued.

私は / できない / 得ることが / 私のカードを / 再発行（の状態）で

I can't get my card reissued **by tomorrow afternoon without the number**.

期限　　　　　条件

35. He is working part-time.

彼は / 最中だ / 働いている / パートで

He is working part-time **to save money to go to a college abroad**.

目的　　　　　目的

36. This instrument is played.

この楽器は / される / 演奏を

This instrument is played **by turning a handle with one hand and pressing keys with the other**.　手段1

手段2

ボキャブラリー the other もう片方

37. It takes him more than 90 minutes to drive.

それは / かからせる / 彼に / 90分以上 / 車で

It takes him more than 90 minutes to drive **from his suburban home to his downtown office**.　出発点

到達点

ボキャブラリー suburban 郊外の　downtown 都心の

38. He has to leave really early.

彼は / しなければならない / 出発することを / かなり早く

He has to leave really early, **for fear of getting caught in backups**.　理由　fear の内容

ボキャブラリー for fear of ～ ～を恐れて、～しないように　get caught in ～ （悪い状態に）おちいる　backups （車の）渋滞

39. The levee was broken.

堤防が / なった / 壊れた（状態に）

The levee was broken **in several places in last night's storm**.　場所　状況

ボキャブラリー levee 堤防

40. The latter's shelf life is long.

後者の消費期限は / 長い

The latter's shelf life is **much** long**er than that of raw fish**.

比較

ボキャブラリー shelf life 棚持ち、消費期限

🔊 **Track 15**

41. Would you prefer to telecommute?

やりたいですか / 在宅勤務を

Would you prefer to telecommute **once a week from next month on**?

頻度　　　(始まりの) 時期

ボキャブラリー telecommute 在宅勤務をする

42. I drove my car back.

私は / 運転した / 自分の車を / 帰る方向へ

I drove my car back **over the bridge into South Carolina**.

越えて　　　　方向

43. We offer them.

我々は / 提供する / それらを

We offer them **for special prices today and tomorrow only**.

価格　　　　期間　　　限定

44. It was being played.

それは / だった / 演奏されている最中

It was being played **by a street musician on the street in Madrid**.

行為者　　　　　場所　場所

45. The swindlers trick gullible old people.

詐欺師たちは / だます / だまされやすい年配の人々を

The swindlers trick gullible old people **into sending money to them**. 結果

(ボキャブラリー) swindler 詐欺師　gullible だまされやすい

46. They chose three plans.

彼らは / 選んだ / 3つのプランを

They chose three plans **out of ten on the basis of their sales figures**. 数量　土台、基盤　土台の内容

(ボキャブラリー) out of ～ ～の中から　on the basis of ～ ～に基づいて
sales figures 売り上げ額

47. You make mortgage payments.

あなたは / おこなう / 住宅ローンの支払いを

You make mortgage payments **instead of throwing away money on rent**. 前の内容との対比

(ボキャブラリー) mortgage 住宅ローン　instead of ～ ～ではなく

061

48. You can achieve your goal.

あなたは / 達成できる / あなたの目標を

You can achieve your goal **with a little more elbow grease**. 条件（もう少し努力すれば）

49. Ted took a walk.

Ted は / した / 散歩を

Ted took a walk **down the street to the park to get refreshed**. 方向　到達点　目的

50. Jake suddenly fell.

    Jake は / 急に / 落ちた

Jake suddenly fell **off the bike halfway down the block**.

                      分離（落ちて）   地点   場所、方向

ボキャブラリー   block（都市の）一区画、街区

2. 名詞の修飾のリスニング

▶ 練習の手順

基本形 の練習は〈1. センテンスの修飾のリスニング〉と同じです。
基本形＋修飾語 には修飾される名詞と修飾語に、英語の語順で日本語訳
が示されています。

音声は各センテンスを3回くり返します。

1. 英文を見て音声を聞きます。名詞と修飾語の語順を意識します。日本語
   では名詞を前から説明しますが、英語は後ろからなので英語の語順で理
   解するようにします。

2. 英文を見ながら音声に合わせて発音します。名詞を後ろから説明する語
   順に慣れるようにします。

3. 英文を見ないで音声を聞いて、語順を意識して英文を言います。

例：The man studying the Japanese literature visited
    男性 / 勉強している / 日本文学を

an old temple in Kyoto.
    古いお寺 / 京都の

---

1. James won the speech contest.

   ジェームスは / 優勝した / スピーチコンテストで

   James won <u>the speech contest</u> **for foreigners**.

   スピーチコンテスト / 外国人のための

2. He made a speech.

   彼は / おこなった / スピーチを

   He made <u>a speech</u> **about an American woman traveling around Japan**.

   スピーチ / アメリカ人女性についての / 日本中を旅した

3. The prize was a trip.

   賞品は / 旅行だった

   The prize was <u>a trip</u> **to Hokkaido for five days**.

   旅行 / 北海道への / 五日間の

4. I'd like to make a reservation.

   私は / したい / 予約を

   I'd like to make <u>a reservation</u> **for Friday night for three**.

   予約　　　　　金曜の夜の　　　3人の

5. He gets double.

   彼は / 稼いでいる / 2倍

   He gets <u>double</u> **what I get**.

   2倍 / 私が稼ぐ（お金の）

6. Salmon pasta is an expensive choice.

サーモンパスタは / 高価なチョイスだ

Salmon pasta **with salad** is a **more** expensive choice **than pepperoncino**.

サーモンパスタ / サラダ付きの / もっと ペペロンチーノより

7. The man works for a publishing company.

その男性は / 働いている / 出版社で

The man **named Tim** works for a publishing company **in Shinjuku**.

その男性 / Tim という名の　　　　　　出版社　　　/ 新宿の

8. The bridge is a famous tourist attraction.

その橋は / 有名な観光名所だ

The bridge **built over that river** is a famous tourist attraction.

橋 / その川にかけられた

064

9. Sophie dropped her camera.

Sophie は / 落とした / 彼女のカメラを

Sophie dropped her camera **her grandfather had bought her**.

彼女のカメラ / おじいさんが買ってくれた

10. Taro looked up English words in a dictionary.

太郎は / 探した / 英語の単語を / 辞書で

Taro looked up English words **he didn't understand** in a dictionary.

英単語 / 彼が理解できない

11. Ami bought her niece a book.

明末は / 買ってあげた / 姪に / 本を

Ami bought her niece a book **with cute pictures, written in easy English**.　本 / かわいい絵がある / 簡単な英語で

書かれている

12. It's about time.

そろそろ / 時間だ

It's about time **we upgraded our OS**.

時間 / 我々が OS をアップグレードすべき

13. The woman came up to the man.

女性が / 近づいてきた / 男性に

The woman **in a blue dress** came up to the man **with glasses**.

女性 / 青いドレスを着た　　　　　　　男性 / メガネをかけた

14. His attempt ended up failing.

彼の試みは / 終わった / 失敗して

His attempt **to swim across the Channel for France** ended up failing.　彼の試み / 英仏海峡を泳いで渡る / フランスへ

ボキャブラリー　the Channel ドーバー海峡、英仏海峡

15. I hope you've all had a chance.

私は / 望む / 皆さんが / 持ったことを / チャンスを

I hope you've all had a chance **to look at the bar chart our department has handed out**.　チャンス / 棒グラフを見る / 我が

部が配布した

16. I don't think we can find another restaurant.

私は / 思わない / 私たちができると / 見つけること / 他のレストランを

I don't think we can find another restaurant **to our taste**.

他のレストラン / 口に合った

17. Please go to the security office.

どうぞ / 行ってください / 警備室へ

Please go to the security office **by the north elevators in the basement**.

警備室 / 北エレベーター横の / 地下の

18. I'm not promising that you'll get everything.

私は / 約束しない / あなた方が / 得ることを / すべてを

I'm not promising that you'll get everything **you ask for**.

すべてのこと / あなた方が求める

19. The sales reps will meet any request.

営業社員たちは / 合わせる / どのような要望にも

The sales reps **from D Corp**. will meet any request **you make**.

営業社員たち / D Corp. 社の / あらゆる要望 / あなたが出す

20. I'm calling about the position.

私は / 電話しています / 仕事について

I'm calling about the position **you interviewed for last week**.

仕事 / あなたが（そのため）面接を受けた / 先週

ボキャブラリー position 職、仕事

21. This fish market sells a variety of fish.

この魚市場は / 売る / いろいろな魚を

This fish market sells a variety of fish **caught or farmed locally**.

いろいろな魚 / 地元で捕獲か養殖された

ボキャブラリー　farm 耕す、(家畜を) 育てる、養殖する

22. The basic rights of these people must be protected by law.

この人々の基本的権利は / 守られなければならない / 法律で

The basic rights of these people **trying to escape poverty** must be protected by law. この人々の / 貧困を抜け出そうとしている

23. Keiko is a working mother.

圭子は / である / ワーキングマザー

Keiko is a working mother **with a baby boy**.

ワーキングマザーだ / 男の赤ちゃんがいる

24. We should promote sales for the one.

我々は / 促進すべきだ / 販売を / それの

We should promote sales for the one **selling the second most this quarter**. それ / 2番目によく売れている / この四半期に

25. I'm waiting for a call from the client.

私は待っています / 電話を / クライアントからの

I'm waiting for a call from the client **I told you about yesterday**.

クライアント / 私があなたに言った / 昨日

26. I need to call a client.

私は / 必要だ / 電話することが / クライアントに

I need to call a client **I'm meeting with today**.

クライアントに / 私が会う予定の / 今日

27. Keisuke is a college student.

圭介は / 大学生だ

Keisuke is a college student **who majors in international relations**.

大学生 / 専攻している / 国際関係を

28. He is interested in studying in a country.

彼は / 興味がある / 勉強することに / 国で

He is interested in studying in a country **where English is its official language**.

国 / そこでは / 英語が公用語だ

29. There are some symptoms.

ある / いくつかの症状が

There are some symptoms **which occur in the first stage of the disease**.

いくつかの症状 / 起こる / 最初の段階で / その病気の

30. Many celebrities feel friendship for the actor.

多くの有名人が / 感じている / 親しみを / その俳優に

Many celebrities **from the country** feel friendship for the actor.

多くの有名人 / その国出身の

🔊 **Track 19**

31. Dr. Smith is a biologist.

Smith 教授は / である / 生物学者

Dr. Smith is a biologist **specializing in immunology**.

生物学者 / 専門にしている / 免疫学を

32. He helps out at the traditional Japanese inn.

彼は / 手伝う / 伝統的な日本式の宿を

He helps out at the traditional Japanese inn **his wife's family runs**.　伝統的な日本式の宿 / 彼の妻の家族が経営する

33. The record-breaking storm has left behind tremendous destruction.

記録破りの嵐が / 残した / すさまじい破壊を

The record-breaking storm has left behind tremendous destruction, **which could mean years of rebuilding**.

すさまじい破壊 / それは意味するかもしれない / 数年の再建を

34. A heavy truck exploded into flames.

大型トラックが / 爆発した / 炎の中へと（炎上した）

A heavy truck **carrying tons of electric wires** exploded into flames.　大型トラック / 積んだ / 何トンもの電線を

ボキャブラリー　explode into flames 爆発炎上する

35. It's easy to tell a horse from a zebra.

それは簡単だ / （それとは）区別すること / 馬を / シマウマと

It's easy to tell a horse from a zebra, **which has black-and-white stripes**.　シマウマ / それは持っている / 白黒の縞模様を

36. It's easy to tell a zebra from another zebra.

それは簡単だ / （それとは）区別すること / シマウマを / 別のシマウマと

It's easy to tell a zebra from another zebra **which has its young**.

別なシマウマ / それは持っている / 子供を

ボキャブラリー　young 動物や鳥の子供（集合名詞）

37. The down time is quite limited.

休暇は / 限られている

The down time **you can take during the first year** is quite limited. 休暇 / あなたが取れる / 1年目に

（ボキャブラリー） down time 休暇

38. The company needed an additional budget.

その会社は / 必要とした / 追加予算を

The company needed an additional budget **equal to its total labor cost**. 追加予算 / 同等の / その総人件費と

（ボキャブラリー） labor cost 人件費

39. The mountain is Mt. Fuji.

その山は / 富士山です

The mountain **visible in the distance** is Mt. Fuji. その山 / 見える / 遠くに

40. No one can ride this attraction.

誰もできない / 乗ることが / このアトラクションに

Anyone **whose height is below 130 centimeters can't** ride this attraction. 誰でも / その身長が / 130cm 以下　できない

🔊 Track 20

41. We sell used cars between five and ten years old.

我々は / 売る / 中古車を / 5年から10年落ちの

We sell used cars between five and ten years old **that are in good condition**. 中古車 / 5年から10年落ちの / それらは良い状態の

42. I often browse the popular websites.

私は / しばしば / 閲覧する / 人気があるウェブサイトを

I often browse the popular websites **featuring the latest fashion trends**. 人気があるウェブサイト / 特に扱っている / 最新のファッショントレンドを

ボキャブラリー　feature 特集する

43. I can recommend some hotels.

私は / 推薦できる / いくつかのホテルを

I can recommend some hotels **for you to stay at with your family**. いくつかのホテル / あなたが / 滞在する / 家族と一緒に

44. There are some problems.

ある / いくつかの問題が

There are some problems **for us to talk about during the meeting**. いくつかの問題 / 我々が / 議論すべき / 会議で

45. The one is serving us well.

それは / 役立っている / 我々に / すごく

The one **we're using** is serving us well.
それ / 我々が使っている

46. It's Ok whenever I can get a good deal.

いつでも大丈夫 / 私が / 得られるなら / 良い取引を

It's OK whenever I can get a good deal **on flights and hotels after Easter**. 良い取引 / フライトとホテルで / 復活祭の後

ボキャブラリー　Easter 復活祭（キリスト教の祭日）

47. The secretary takes care of all of his appointments.

秘書が / 管理している / 彼のすべてのアポイントを

The secretary **to Mr. Douglas** takes care of all of his appointments.

秘書が / Mr. Douglas の

48. Our discussion shouldn't only be based on online information.

我々の議論は / べきでない / もとづく / ネットの情報だけに

Our discussion **on politics** shouldn't only be based on online

我々の議論 / 政治に関する　　　　　　　　　　　　　ネットの

information **available to anyone**.

情報　　　 / 入手可能な / 誰にでも

49. John decided to sell the pottery.

John は / 決めた / 売ることを / 陶磁器を

John decided to sell the pottery **that has been passed down**

from his ancestors.　　　陶磁器を　　　 / 受け継がれてきた

　　　 / 祖先から

ボキャブラリー　　pass down 受け継ぐ、引き継ぐ

50. The customer complained about the laptop.

その客は / クレームをつけた / ノートパソコンに

The customer complained about the laptop **she had recently**

bought at the store.　　　　　　　　　　ノートパソコン / 彼女が最近買

った / 　　その店で

072

練習問題

音声は途中で止めずに聞いてください。どの問題も1問正解ごとに1点ですが、繰り返し聞くごとに0.2点引いてください。何回も聞けば得点がマイナスになります。

1. 各空所に人、場所などの選択肢が2つずつあります。音声を聞いて正しい方を選んでください。

> 例：（⓪人・物）（現在・⓪過去）（⓪場所・時間）（場所・⓪時間）
> 【音声】 The students | came | to school | yesterday .

🔊 **Track 21**

1)（人・物）（現在・過去）（人・物）（目的・場所）

2)（物・出来事）（回数・頻度）（現在・過去）（場所・時間）

3)（人・物）（現在・過去）（人・手段）（場所・時間）

4)（人・物）（現在・未来）（手段・時間）（手段・場所）

5)（人・物）（未来・過去）（話題・時間）

6)（人・物）（現在・過去）（人・事柄）（場所・分野）

7)（人・場所）（現在・過去）（人・物）（時間・目的）

8)（人・物）（現在・過去）（人・物）（代理・相手）

9)（人・物）（現在・過去）（人・物）

10)（人・物）（未来・現在）（人・物）

2. 音声を聞いて空所に修飾語を入れてください。場所、時間など、情報の種類をヒントとして示します。

例：Ted made a presentation ＿＿＿＿＿＿ ＿＿＿＿＿＿.
　　　　　　　　　　　　　　　　 相手　　　　　　　場所
【音声】Ted made a presentation to his clients in Conference Room1.

🔊 **Track 22**

1) Children learn many things ＿＿＿＿＿＿ ＿＿＿＿＿＿.
　　　　　　　　　　　　　　　　　　 手段　　　　　　　場所

2) Dr. Russell delivered a lecture ＿＿＿＿＿＿ ＿＿＿＿＿＿.
　　　　　　　　　　　　　　　　　　　 題材　　　　　　　頻度

3) Jean walked ＿＿＿＿＿＿ ＿＿＿＿＿＿ ＿＿＿＿＿＿.
　　　　　　　　 方向　　　　　 到達点　　　　　 人

4) Some people commute ＿＿＿＿＿＿ ＿＿＿＿＿＿.
　　　　　　　　　　　　　　 手段　　　　　　　時・日

5) We have to drive ＿＿＿＿＿＿ ＿＿＿＿＿＿.
　　　　　　　　　　 通過　　　　　　　到達点

6) She went ＿＿＿＿＿＿ ＿＿＿＿＿＿.
　　　　　　 到達点　　　　　　　目的

7) You are required to keep your bags _____

_____ .

場所

時間

8) Many ships were sunk _____ _____ .

場所　　　　　　　　位置（離れて）

9) They should look into customer feedback _____

_____ .

時間

目的

10) Cindy and Tom talked _____

_____ .

話題

時間

3. 音声を聞いて空所に名詞＋修飾語を入れてください。日本語訳をヒントにできますが、英語の語順通りではありません。

🔊 Track 23

1) _____ has to get up at five to prepare their box lunches.

その3人の子持ちのお母さんは、彼らの弁当を準備するために5時に起きないといけない。

2) I'm waiting for a call from _____ .

昨日言ったクライアントからの電話を待っています。

3) Mr. Robertson must be _____ .

Mr. Robertson は我々の未来にとって一番の選択に違いない。

4) The president is to announce a restructuring plan in

_____.

社長は、明日行われる会議で再建プランを発表する予定だ。

ボキャブラリー be to ～ ～する予定だ

5) I saw _____ derailed.

私はガソリンを積んでいる電車が脱線するのを見た。

ボキャブラリー derailed 脱線した

6) _____ was not very long.

Sandra が取った休暇は、すごく長くはなかった。

7) Would you like to change _____?

あなたの仕事のスタイルを何か変えたいですか？

8) _____ say a lot about you.

あなたが持っている考え（見解）はあなたについて多くを語ります。

9) _____ is tacky, I think.

私は、あなたが誕生日プレゼントで彼女にあげた指輪はダサいと思います。

ボキャブラリー tacky（口語）ダサい

10) As for _____, we can discuss it in the future.

アジアで働くというあなたの希望（要求）に関しては、将来話し合えます。

ボキャブラリー as for ～ ～に関しては

4. 音声を聞いて内容と合う選択肢を A、B から選んで○で囲んでください。

例：【音声】Ted answered the phone for Mr. Thompson.
　　【選択肢】A. Ted talked with Mr. Thompson on the phone.
　　　　　　　B. Ted didn't talk with Mr. Thompson on the phone.
　　【訳】Ted は Mr. Thompson の代わりに電話に出た。
　　　　　A. Ted は Mr. Thompson と電話で話した。
　　　　　B. Ted は Mr. Thompson と電話で話さなかった。
　　【答】A Ⓑ
　　for Mr. Thompson = Mr. Thompson に代わって

🔊 **Track 24**

1) A. Kaori crossed the river.
　 B. Kaori didn't cross the river.
　 答：A　B

2) A. The local people have an opportunity to learn about the history once a week.
　 B. Dr. Farmer loves to visit historical sites with those in the neighborhood.
　 答：A　B

3) A. Travel magazines write about travelers visiting local eateries.
　 B. Travel magazines write about food served locally.
　 答：A　B

4) A. The CEO had trouble remembering his clients.
　 B. The CEO met many people just after he got his position.
　 答：A　B

5) A. Some children may unknowingly become criminals.
   B. Some children are familiar with Internet crimes.
   答：A B

6) A. Haon studied in London until her 30th birthday.
   B. Haon studied abroad until she was over twenty thanks to her family.
   答：A B

7) A. Ted's colleagues spoke well of him.
   B. Julius asked Ted's colleagues if he is an accountant.
   答：A B

8) A. Carl was absent from work to go to a place away from home.
   B. Carl visited his grandparents for three days.
   答：A B

9) A. Bob's wife wanted him to go to the supermarket.
   B. Bob likes to go to the supermarket with his wife.
   答：A B

10) A. Not all people trust the government for all it says.
    B. The government is supposed to know the problem everyone has.
    答：A B

正解 ＿＿＿＿ 問 － （聞き返し＿＿＿ 回 × 0.2） = ＿＿＿＿ 点
満点　40点

解答

1.

1)（<u>人</u>・物）（現在・<u>過去</u>）（<u>人</u>・物）（<u>目的</u>・場所）

| James | met with | a client | to discuss the next year's plan |.

James は / 会った / クライアントに / 次の年のプランを話し合うために

2)（物・<u>出来事</u>）（回数・<u>頻度</u>）（<u>現在</u>・過去）（<u>場所</u>・時間）

| Traffic accidents | sometimes | happen | at the intersection |.

交通事故が / 時々 / 起こる / この交差点で

3)（人・<u>物</u>）（現在・<u>過去</u>）（<u>人</u>・手段）（<u>場所</u>・時間）

| Those ships | were attacked | by the pirates | on their return trip |.

これらの船は / 攻撃された / 海賊によって / 帰る道で

079

4)（<u>人</u>・物）（現在・<u>未来</u>）（<u>手段</u>・時間）（手段・<u>場所</u>）

| More and more people | will work | online | from home |.

ますます多くの人が / 働くだろう / オンラインで / 家から

5)（<u>人</u>・物）（未来・<u>過去</u>）（<u>話題</u>・時間）

| Both sides | agreed | on the deadline |.

両者は / 同意した / 締め切りに関して

6)（<u>人</u>・物）（<u>現在</u>・過去）（人・<u>事柄</u>）（場所・<u>分野</u>）

| The critic | highly evaluates | John's contribution |
| to European art |.

その批評家は / 高く評価する / John の貢献を / ヨーロッパ芸術に対する

7) (人 ・場所) (現在 ・過去) (人 ・物) (時間 ・目的)

The artist from Japan | has helped | the local artists | for years .

その日本出身のアーティストは / 助けてきた / 地元の芸術家たちを / 何年も

8) (人 ・物) (現在・ 過去) (人・ 物) (代理 ・相手)

The politician | answered | the phone | for Mr. Jackson .

その政治家は / 出た / 電話に / Mr. Jackson の代わりに

9) (人 ・物) (現在 ・過去) (人・ 物)

The teacher with a red tie | loves

the bag his wife bought for him .

その赤いネクタイの教師は / 好きだ / 彼の奥さんが買ってくれたバッグが

10) (人 ・物) (未来・ 現在) (人・ 物)

Many movie lovers | browse

the websites featuring movie stars .

多くの映画愛好家は / 閲覧する / 映画スターを特集したウェブサイトを

2.

1) Children learn many things through repetition at school and home.

子供たちは / 学ぶ / 多くのことを / 反復を通して / 学校と家で

2) Dr. Russell delivered a lecture on French history every week.

Russel 教授は / おこなった / 講義を / フランス史に関して / 毎週

3) Jean walked down the street to the supermarket with her son.

Jean は / 歩いた / 通りを下って / スーパーマーケットへ / 息子と

4) Some people commute in their cars on rainy days.

ある人々は / 通勤する / 自分の車で / 雨の日は

5) We have to drive <u>over the mountain</u> to the village.

我々は / 車で行かないといけない / 山を越えて / その村へ

6) She went <u>to her mother's house</u> to help her clean her house.

彼女は / 行った / お母さんの家に / 家を掃除する手伝いをするために

7) You are required to keep your bags <u>in the overhead compartment</u> <u>during the flight</u>.

あなたは / 必要だ / 保つことが / カバンを / 頭上の荷物入れに / 飛行中は

8) Many ships were sunk <u>near the island</u> <u>off the east coast</u>.

多くの船が / 沈没した / 島の近くで / 東海岸沖の

9) They should look into customer feedback <u>before the next meeting</u> <u>to make a new plan</u>.

081

彼らは / 調べるべきだ / 顧客のフィードバックを / 次の会議の前に / 新しい計画の作成のために

10) Cindy and Tom talked <u>about their son's performance at school</u> <u>the day before yesterday</u>.

Cindy と Tom は / 話し合った / 息子の学校での成績について / おととい

3.
1) The mother with three children
2) the client I told you about yesterday
3) the best choice for our future
4) the meeting to be held tomorrow
5) a train carrying gasoline

6) The vacation Sandra took

7) anything about your working style

8) The opinions you hold

9) The ring you gave her for a birthday present

10) your request to work in Asia

4.

1) 答：B

スクリプト

Kaori was walking along the river to see Keiko.

A. Kaori crossed the river.

B. Kaori didn't cross the river.

訳

佳織は圭子に会うために川に沿って歩いていた。

A. 佳織は川を渡った。

B. 佳織は川を渡らなかった。

2) 答：A

スクリプト

Dr. Farmer gives talks on the local history to those living in the neighborhood on Saturdays.

A. The local people have an opportunity to learn about the history once a week.

B. Dr. Farmer loves to visit historical sites with those in the neighborhood.

訳

Farmer 教授は土曜日に近所の人々に地元の歴史について話す。

A. 地元の人々は週一回歴史について学ぶ機会がある。

B. Farmer 教授は近所の人々と史跡を訪ねることが好きだ。

3) 答：B

Some travelers love to visit the local eateries travel magazines frequently feature.

A. Travel magazines write about travelers visiting local eateries.

B. Travel magazines write about food served locally.

訳

ある旅行者たちは、旅行雑誌が頻繁に特集する地元の食べ物屋さんを訪ねることが好きだ。

A. 旅行雑誌は地元の食べ物屋を訪ねる旅行者について書く。

B. 旅行雑誌は地元で提供される食べ物について書く。

ボキャブラリー eatery 食べ物屋さん、レストラン、食堂

4) 答：B

スクリプト

The new CEO met with more clients during his first two months to have them remember him.

A. The CEO had trouble remembering his clients.

B. The CEO met many people just after he got his position.

訳

その新 CEO は最初の 2 ヵ月間、顔を覚えてもらうためにより多くのクライアントに会った。

A. CEO はクライアントを覚えることに苦労した。

B. CEO はその地位に就いた直後、多くの人と会った。

5) 答：A

スクリプト

In today's digital world, there is a chance that ordinary children will become involved in criminal acts only by connecting with strangers on the Internet.

A. Some children may unknowingly become criminals.

B. Some children are familiar with Internet crimes.

訳

今日のデジタル世界では、普通の子供たちがインターネットで他人と接続するだけで、犯罪行為に巻き込まれる可能性がある。

A. ある子供たちは知らない間に犯罪者になるかもしれない。

B. ある子供たちはインターネット犯罪に精通している。

6) 答：B

スクリプト

Haon came from a wealthy family. She had been educated in London until she was twenty-two and came back home to Seoul after her 30th birthday.

A. Haon studied in London until her 30th birthday.

B. Haon studied abroad until she was over twenty thanks to her family.

訳

ハオンは裕福な家に生まれた。彼女は22歳までLondonで勉強して、30歳の誕生日を迎えたあとでソウルに帰ってきた。

A. ハオンは30歳の誕生日までLondonで勉強した。

B. ハオンは家族のおかげで20歳を越えるまで海外で勉強した。

7) 答：A

スクリプト

Julius heard some good things about Ted as an accountant from other members in the accounting department.

A. Ted's colleagues spoke well of him.

B. Julius asked Ted's colleagues if he is an accountant.

訳

Juliusは経理部の他のメンバーから、会計士としてのTedの良いこと

を聞いた。

A. Ted の同僚たちは彼を誉めた。

B. Julius は Ted の同僚に彼が会計士かどうか聞いた。

ボキャブラリー speak well of ～ ～の良いことを言う、誉める　cf. speak ill of ～ ～の悪口を言う

8) **答：A.**

スクリプト

Carl took a day off from work three days ago to visit his grandparents who are living far away from him.

A. Carl was absent from work to go to a place away from home.

B. Carl visited his grandparents for three days.

訳

Carl は3日前、遠くに住む祖父母を訪ねるために仕事を休んだ。

A. Carl は家から遠くの、ある場所へ行くために仕事を休んだ。

B. Carl は祖父母を3日間訪ねた。

9) **答：A**

スクリプト

Bob didn't feel like driving to the supermarket for his wife, only to buy one pack of beef.

A. Bob's wife wanted him to go to the supermarket.

B. Bob likes to go to the supermarket with his wife.

訳

Bob は牛肉を1パック買うだけのために、妻に代わってスーパーへ行く気がしなかった。

A. Bob の妻は彼にスーパーへ行ってほしかった。

B. Bob は妻とスーパーへ行くのが好きだ。

10) **答：A**

Some say there are problems with the way the government treats the official information everyone is supposed to know.

A. Not all people trust the government for all it says.

B. The government is supposed to know the problem everyone has.

訳

ある人々は、誰もが知る権利がある公的情報に対する政府の扱い方に問題があると考えている。

A. 政府が言うことを誰もが信じているわけではない。

B. 政府は誰もが持っている問題を知っていると思われている。

ボキャブラリー　be supposed to (do) 〜だと思われている、〜のはずだろう

Part 2
名詞節を含むリスニング

英文が長くなる要因のひとつは節（主語、動詞を含む語の集まり）が含まれている場合です。ひとつの文で複数の主語や動詞があるのでリスニングが難しくなります。特に、節になった主語や目的語を聞き取れることがリスニング上達には必須です。主語や目的語になる節は名詞節と呼ばれ、**that**節と間接疑問文に分けられます。

※ that 節には、名詞の説明をする「同格の that」と呼ばれるパターンも含みます。詳しくは〈1. that 節を含むリスニング〉で説明します。

Part 2の構成

Part 2 は〈1. that 節を含むリスニング〉と〈2. 間接疑問文を含むリスニング〉があります。Part 1 は 基本形 + 修飾語 の構成でしたが、that 節や間接疑問文は主語や目的語の位置にはめ込まれるので、Part 2 は 基本形 + 基本形はめ込み文 になります。

---

1. that 節

基本形

Mark needs help.

Mark は / 必要だ / 助けが

↓

基本形はめ込み文

Someone says that Mark needs help.

誰かが言っている / Mark は助けが必要だと

2. 疑節疑問文

基本形

Is Mr. Hill married?

しているの？ / Hill 氏は / 結婚を

↓

基本形はめ込み文

Nobody knows if Mr. Hill is married.

誰も知らない / Hill 氏が結婚しているかどうか

＊間接疑問文は肯定文の語順になり、クエスチョンマークも付けません。

練習の手順

音声は各センテンスを3回繰り返します。

まず、基本形の練習をします。英文の下に英語の語順で日本語訳があります。

1. 英語を見て音声を聞きます。この時、日本語を参考にして英語の語順で英文を理解します。
2. 英文を見て音声に合わせて発音します。日本語は見ません。
3. 英文を見ないで音声を聞いた後に、語順を意識して英文を言います。

基本形に続いて基本形はめ込み文の練習をします。

1. 英語を見て音声を聞きます。この時、日本語を参考にして英語の語順で英文を理解します。
2. 英文を見て音声に合わせて発音します。日本語は見ません。
3. 英文を見ないで音声を聞いた後に、語順を意識して英文を言います。基本形が主語、目的語のどの位置にはめ込まれたか、または名詞の説明なのかを意識してください。

1. that 節のリスニング

ここで練習する that 節は次の通りです。

1) Yoshikazu knows (that) Mika is a sincere woman.
良和は / 知っている / 美香が誠実な女性であることを
▶ 下線部が動詞 know の目的語。that は省略可

2) It is understandable that Yoshikazu loves Mika.
それは / 理解できる / (それとは) 良和が愛している / 美香を
▶ It... that 構文。that 以下の下線部が主語で It は仮主語

3) There is a general agreement that the world has warmed slightly over the past 100 years or so.
一般的な合意がある / 世界が少し暖かくなったという (合意) / 過去100年くらいで
▶ 下線部が名詞 agreement の内容。文法上の名前は「同格の that」

◆ 注意
「同格の that」は文の主語や目的語になるのではなく名詞を修飾するので part 1の名詞の修飾に分類可能ですが、名詞節なので that 節のグループとして part 2に含みます。

🔊 Track 25

1. Josh had visited Japan before.
Josh は / 訪ねたことがあった / 日本を / 以前
No one told me Josh had visited Japan before.
誰も言わなかった / 私に / Josh が訪ねたことがあると / 日本を / 以前

2. You are here for your checkup.

あなたは / ここに来ている / 健康診断で

Your chart says that you are here for your checkup.

あなたのカルテに / 書いてある / あなたはここに来ていると / 健康診断で

3. The business owner found that there was a tendency.

そのビジネスオーナーは / 発見した / 傾向があることを

The business owner found that there was a tendency **that their loyal customers buy more chicken than pork**.

そのビジネスオーナーは / 発見した / 傾向があることを / 彼らの常連客は / 買うという（傾向）/ 豚肉よりも鶏肉を

4. He gets double what I get.

彼は / もらっている / 2倍 / 私がもらっている分の

I happened to find out he gets double what I get.

私は偶然に知った / 彼は / もらっている / 2倍 / 私がもらっている分の

5. Our program could be too demanding for some students.

我々のプログラムは / かもしれない / 要求が高すぎる / ある学生たちには

It is possible that our program could be too demanding for some students.

それは可能性がある /（それとは）我々のプログラムは要求が高すぎる / ある学生たちには

6. Their local staff have quite a high level of expertise.

彼らの地元スタッフは / 持っている / すごく高いレベルを / 専門知識の

I've read their local staff have quite a high level of expertise.

私は読んだ / 彼らの地元スタッフは / 持っている / すごく高いレベルを / 専門知識の

ボキャブラリー expertise 専門知識

7. A rumor spread.

噂が / 広まった

A [rumor] spread **that Flight Airlines had sold out to a competitor**.

噂が広まった /（噂とは）Flight Airlines が / 身売りした / ライバルに

◆ ワンポイントアドバイス

7のように同格の that 節が長く述語以降が短い場合は、that 節が説明する名詞（ここでは rumor）と離れて述語の後ろに来ます。

8. The billing address the customer gave us must be wrong.

請求書発送用住所 / そのお客さんがくれた / 〜は違いない / 間違いに

Our accounting department found that the billing address the customer gave us must be wrong.

我々の経理部が見つけた / 請求書発送用住所 / そのお客さんがくれた / 〜は違いない / 間違いに

(ボキャブラリー) billing 請求書の作成や発送

9. Cultural exchanges between the two nations will be expanded.

文化交流 / 2か国間の / 〜は拡大されるだろう

It is likely that cultural exchanges between the two nations will be expanded.

それはありそうだ /（それとは）2か国間の文化交流の機会が拡大されること

10. Brandon had quit his job.

Brandon は辞めていた / 彼の仕事を

Nobody knew Brandon had quit his job.

誰も知らなかった / Brandon が仕事を辞めていたことを

2. 間接疑問文のリスニング

ここで練習する間接疑問文は次の通りです。

---

1) Yoshikazu knows how sincere Mika is.

良和は / 知っている / どれほど誠実であるか / 美香が

▶ 下線部が動詞 know の目的語

2) How you study at school can determine your future success.

どのようにあなたが学校で学ぶかは / 決めるかもしれない / 将来の成功を

▶ 下線部が主語

3) I am interested in who can best run this system.

私は興味がある / 誰が最もうまく動かせるか / このシステムを

▶ 下線部が前置詞 in の目的語

4) It is questionable how much Japanese Jack can learn in a month.

それは疑わしい / (それとは) どれほどの日本語を / Jack が習得できるか / 1 か月で

▶ 間接疑問文も It...that 構文のように仮主語 it を取る

🔊 **Track 26**

1. Which color do you prefer?

どの色をあなたは（より）好きですか？

Could you tell me which color you prefer?

言ってもらえますか？ / 私に / どの色を / あなたは / （より）好きか

2. Why does Canada have two official languages?

なぜ / カナダは持っているの？ / 2つの公用語を

You said you would research why Canada has two official languages.

あなたは言った / 研究すると / なぜ / カナダは持っているか / 2つの公用語を

3. What is the market value of this old stamp?

何が / 市場価格ですか？ / この古い切手の

There is no general agreement on what the market value of this old stamp is.

ない / 一般的な合意は / 〜に関して / 何が市場価格か / この古い切手の

4. How much would you like to exchange?

いくら / したいですか？ / 交換を

Could you write down here how much you'd like to exchange?

書いていただけますか？ / ここに / いくらしたいか / 交換を

5. How can he get promoted?

いかにして / できるか？ / 彼は / 昇進を

Mr. Atkinson always thinks about how he can get promoted.

Mr. Atkinson は / いつも考えている / 〜について / いかに / 彼が昇進できるか

6. What can slow down global warming?

何が / 遅くさせられるか / 地球温暖化を

Today, more people are interested in what can slow down global warming **than a decade ago**.

今日、より多くの人が興味を持っている / 何が遅くさせられるかに / 地球温暖化を / 10年前より

7. What percentage of the population speaks two languages?

どれほどの割合が / 人口の / 話すか？ / 2 か国語を

The question arose as to what percentage of the population speaks two languages.

質問（疑問）が / 生じた / 〜に関して / 人口のどれほどの割合が / 話すかという / 2 か国語を

ボキャブラリー as to 〜 〜に関しては

8. When and where would he go for a vacation?

いつ、どこへ / でしょう？ / 彼は / 行く / 休暇で

Leslie was thinking about when and where he would go for a vacation.

Leslie は / 考えていた / 〜について / いつ、どこへ / 彼は / 行く / 休暇で

9. How excited they are during the World Series!（感嘆文）

どれほどワクワクするか！ / 彼らは / ワールドシリーズの間

Matilda and Tony talked about how excited they are during the World Series.

Matilda と Tony は / 話した / 〜について / どれほどワクワクするか / ワールドシリーズの間

10. What is the problem and how should it be solved?

何が問題なのか / そして / どのように / されるべきか？ / 解決を

The board of directors should agree on what the problem is and how it should be solved.

取締役会は / 意見一致すべきだ / 〜において / 何が問題なのか / そして / どのように / されるべきか / 解決を

ボキャブラリー board of directors 取締役会

11. Who is Jonathan Swift and when exactly did he live?

誰ですか / Jonathan swift は / そして / いつ / 正確には / 生きましたか？

My knowledge about <u>who Jonathan Swift was and when exactly he lived</u> **is quite limited.**

私の知識 / ～についての / Jonathan Swift は誰か / そして / いつ / 正確には / 生きたか / ～は限られている

ボキャブラリー Jonathan Swift 1667～1745 英国の作家。「ガリバー旅行記」の著者。

12. Can we achieve our quarterly goal?

我々は / 達成できるのか？/ 四半期の目標を

Whether <u>we can achieve our quarterly goal</u> **depends on how well we perform at the beginning.**

達成できるかどうか / 四半期の目標を / ～はかかっている / どれほどうまく / 機能するか / 初期に

13. Who are you and where did you grow up?

誰ですか / あなたは / そして / どこで / 育ったのですか？

You can't be trusted without showing <u>who you are and where you grew up.</u>

あなたは / されない / 信頼を / ～なしでは / 示すことを / だれなのか / あなたは / そして / どこで / 育ったのか

14. What product should we promote most?

どの製品を / すべきか / 我々は / 宣伝を / もっとも

Give me your feedback to help me decide <u>what product we should promote most.</u>

ください / 皆さんのフィードバックを / 私を助けるために / 決めることを / どの製品を / すべきか / 我々は / 宣伝を / もっとも

15. Can Janet speak on such a difficult topic as global warming?

できますか？/ Janet は / 話すことを / 〜について / 難しい題材 / 地球温暖化のような

Everyone in the class wonders if <u>Janet can speak on such a difficult topic as global warming.</u>

全員が / クラス中の / 怪しんでいる / Janet が / 話せるかどうか / 〜について / 難しい題材 / 地球温暖化のような

16. Did he have a job interview with an IT company for an assistant programmer position ?

彼は / 仕事の面接を受けたの？/ IT 企業のアシスタントプログラマー職の

It is uncertain if <u>he had a job interview with an IT company for an assistant programmer position.</u>

それは確かではない / (それというのは) 彼が受けたかどうか / 面接を / IT 企業のアシスタントプログラマー職の

17. Who leads the company?

誰が / 率いるのか？/ 会社を

<u>Who leads the company</u> **will determine the lives of its employees**.

誰が会社を率いるのかは / 決めるだろう / 生活を / 従業員の

18. Do you plan to undertake any professional development?

計画していますか？/ 着手すること / プロの能力開発に

Whether or not <u>you plan to undertake some professional development</u> **may determine your success a decade from now**.

計画するかしないか / 着手する / プロの能力開発に / 決めるかもしれない / あなたの成功を / 今から10年後の

19. How many have already been infected by the virus?

どれくらいの人々が / すでに / 感染したのか？/ そのウィルスに

How many have already been infected by the virus **must be discussed in accordance with scientifically determined criteria**.

どれくらいの人々が / すでに / 感染したのか / そのウィルスに / 議論されなければならない / 〜に従って / 科学的に決定された基準

20. How important is it to keep up with state-of-the-art technologies?

どれほど重要か？ / それは / （それとは）遅れないこと / 最先端技術に

The students in Dr. Smith's lab have a common understanding of how important it is to keep up with state-of-the-art technologies.

Smith 教授の研究室の学生たちは / 持っている / 共通の理解を / どれほど重要かについて / それが / （それとは）遅れないこと / 最先端技術に

ボキャブラリー　state-of-the-art 最新の

練習問題

音声は途中で止めずに聞いてください。どの問題も1問正解ごとに1点ですが、繰り返し聞くごとに0.2点引いてください。何回も聞けば得点がマイナスになります。

◁)) **Track 28**

1. 音声を聞いて空所を埋めてください。日本語訳をヒントにできますが、英語の語順通りではありません。

1) The theory of plate tectonics explains ＿＿＿＿＿＿＿＿＿＿＿＿.
   プレートテクトニクス理論は大陸がどのように動くかを説明する。

2) Edward Jenner is said to have developed ＿＿＿＿＿＿＿＿＿ a vaccine.
   Edward Jenner は、今日ワクチンとして知られているものを開発したと言われている。

3) Thanks to scientific developments, we now have a better understanding of ＿＿＿＿＿＿＿＿＿＿＿＿＿＿.
   科学の発展のおかげで、我々は今日宇宙がどのように創造されたかについて、より理解している。

4) No one can precisely judge ＿＿＿＿＿＿＿＿＿＿＿＿＿ in ten years.
   10年で電気自動車の市場がどれほど大きくなるかは誰も正確には判断できない。

5) The board members met to _____

_____.

取締役会は彼らの新しいビジネスに大きなリスクがあるか確かめるために集まった。

ヒント see if ～ ～かどうか確かめる

6) It appears _____.

我々は教育政策で間違いを犯したように見える。

7) His behavior has made me wonder _____

_____.

彼の行動で、私はチームメンバーが私を信じているか疑いの念を抱いた。

8) It is not surprising that _____.

日本でペット関連の市場が成長し続けているのは驚くべきことではない。

9) Surveillance cameras can help the police determine

_____.

監視カメラは警察がいつどこで犯罪がより起こりやすいかを決める助けをする。

10) Taro is _____ an

archeologist.

太郎はすごく歴史に興味があるので考古学者になりたい。

2. 音声の内容と合う選択肢を A、B から選んで○で囲んでください。

例：【音声】

Jonathan wanted to know why Izabella didn't tell him what she'd got from the merchant.

【選択肢】

A. Jonathan knew that Izabella had bought something from the merchant.

B. Jonathan didn't know that Izabella had bought something from the merchant.

【訳】

Jonathan は Izabella が商人から何を買ったのかを言ってくれない理由を知りたかった。

A. Jonathan は Izabella が商人から何か買ったことを知っていた。

B. Jonathan は Izabella が商人から何か買ったことを知らなかった。

【答】 Ⓐ B

🔊 **Track 29**

1) A. The rescue team knew where in the forest they would find the child.

B. The rescue team knew they could not find the child easily.

答：A　B

2) A. The distance to the school is one thing Marcos thinks matters.

B. The distance and cost depend on how many students will enroll.

答：A　B

3) A. Grace has read books on all topics but ethnology.

B. The books Grace read have likely made her interested in ethnology.

ボキャブラリー　ethnology 民族学、文化人類学

答：A　B

4) A. Kenji made his dog behave well after finding advice on the Internet.

B. Kenji found advice on the way of handling pets on the Internet.

答：A　B

5) A. Misaki is discussing problems of SNS and global warming with international students.

B. Misaki is talking about global warming with different people.

答：A　B

6) A. Becky thinks Harold is very good at getting chances to get married.

B. Harold thinks Becky considers him to be sincere.

答：A　B

7) A. How much they can get next year likely depends on the processing ability of the computer.

B. The budget may differ if the computer is storing much data.

答：A　B

8) A. Justin wanted to see Abbie in the town where she is living.

   B. Abbie wanted to see Justin, but he wasn't at his place.

   答：A　B

9) A. Ai didn't say she wanted to stop playing volleyball.

   B. Ai wanted to go back to the practice because her knee was much better.

   答：A　B

10) A. Ben's adviser tells him to take as many courses as possible as a freshman.

   B. Ben would likely have more opportunity to be an assistant later if he led a lot of outdoor activities.

   答：A　B

正解 _____ 問 － （聞き返し_____ 回 × 0.2) = _____ 点

満点　20点

解答

1.

1) how the continents move

2) what is now known as

3) how the universe was created

4) how large the market for electric cars might be

5) see if there could be a large risk in their new business

6) that we've made a mistake in our education policy

7) whether our team members believe me or not

8) the pet-related market in Japan keeps growing

9) when and where crimes are more likely to occur

10) so interested in history that he wants to be

2.

1) 答：B

スクリプト

The rescue team wondered how deep into the forest they could go to save the lost child.

A. The rescue team knew where in the forest they would find the child.

B. The rescue team knew they could not find the child easily.

訳

レスキュー隊は行方不明の子供を救うためにどれくらい深く森に入らなければならないか分からなかった。

A. レスキュー隊は森のどこで子供を見つけられるか知っていた。

B. レスキュー隊は簡単には子供を見つけられないことを知っていた。

2) 答：A

スクリプト

Which language school Marcos will enroll in depends on how much he should pay for the course and how far he should commute.

A. The distance to the school is one thing Marcos thinks matters.

B. The distance and cost depend on how many students will enroll.

訳

どの語学学校を Marcos が選ぶかは、授業にいくら払うかと、どれくらい遠くまで通学しなければならないかにかかっている。

A. 学校までの距離は Marcos が重要と思っていることのひとつだ。

B. 距離と費用はどれくらい多く学生が入学するかにかかっている。

3) **答：B**

スクリプト

Grace has read so many books about different customs that she is now thinking of studying ethnology.

A. Grace has read books on all topics but ethnology.

B. The books Grace read have likely made her interested in ethnology.

訳

Grace は様々な風習についてたくさんの本を読んだので、今民族学を研究しようと考えている。

A. Grace は様々な本を読んだ。民族学以外は。

B. Grace が読んだ本で、おそらく彼女は民族学に興味を持ったようだ。

4) **答：B**

スクリプト

Kenji found a website for dog lovers. There, he found advice on how pet owners can train their pets to behave well.

A. Kenji made his dog behave well after finding advice on the

Internet.

B. Kenji found advice on the way of handling pets on the Internet.

訳

健司は犬好きのためのウェブサイトを見つけた。そのサイトで彼は、ペットオーナーがどのようにして自分のペットの行儀を良くする訓練ができるかについてのアドバイスを見つけた。

A. 健司はインターネットでアドバイスを見つけた後、彼の犬の行儀をよくした。

B. 健司はペットを扱う方法についてのアドバイスをインターネットで見つけた。

5) **答：B**

スクリプト

Misaki is thinking about what she can do to slow down global warming. She has been discussing this problem with high school students from different countries on SNS.

A. Misaki is discussing problems of SNS and global warming with international students.

B. Misaki is talking about global warming with different people.

訳

美咲は地球温暖化を遅らせるために自分に何ができるか考えている。彼女は SNS を通して様々な国の高校生とこの問題について議論してきた。

A. 美咲は留学生たちと SNS や地球温暖化の問題を議論している。

B. 美咲は様々な人と地球温暖化について話し合っている。

6) **答：B**

スクリプト

Harold thinks chances are very good that he can get married to Becky, because she always says she likes sincere men.

A. Becky thinks Harold is very good at getting chances to get married.

B. Harold thinks Becky considers him to be sincere.

訳

Harold は Becky と結婚できるチャンスは十分あると思っている。なぜなら彼女は誠実な男性が好きだといつも言っているから。

A. Becky は、Harold が結婚するチャンスをつかむのが上手だと思っている。

B. Harold は Becky が彼のことを誠実だと思っていると考えている。

7) 答：A

スクリプト

How much data this supercomputer can process per minute may determine their budget next year.

A. How much they can get next year likely depends on the processing ability of the computer.

B. The budget may differ if the computer is storing much data.

訳

このスーパーコンピューターが1分あたりどれほどの量のデータを処理できるかで彼らの来年の予算が決まるかもしれない。

A. 彼らが来年いくらもらえるかはコンピューターの処理能力による可能性がある。

B. コンピューターの中にたくさんのデータが入っていれば予算が変わるかもしれない。

8) 答：B

スクリプト

Justin wished Abbie had told him she would visit the town he is living in. He found out afterward she'd wanted to see him during her visit. Unfortunately, he was on a business trip then.

A. Justin wanted to see Abbie in the town where she is living.

106

B. Abbie wanted to see Justin, but he wasn't at his place.

訳

Justin は、Abbie が彼が住んでいる町を訪ねてくることを言っておいてくれていたらと思った。後になって彼は、彼女が訪問中に彼に会いたかったと知った。残念なことに、その時彼は出張中だった。

A. Justin は Abbie が住んでいる町で彼女に会いたかった。

B. Abbie は Justin に会いたかったが、彼は家にいなかった。

9) **答：A**

スプリクト

When Ai's father asked her how her injured knee was, she said it was much better and told him when she would be able to go back to practice. However, that was not what she actually wanted to say. She wanted to quit volleyball.

A. Ai didn't say she wanted to stop playing volleyball.

B. Ai wanted to go back to the practice because her knee was much better.

訳

愛は、ケガしたひざがどうか、父親が聞いた時、かなりいいと答えて、いつ練習に戻られるかを伝えた。しかし、それは彼女が本当に言いたいことではなかった。彼女はバレーボールを辞めたかった。

A. 愛はバレーボールをやめたいと言わなかった。

B. 愛はヒザがかなりよくなったので練習に戻りたかった。

10) **答：B**

スクリプト

Ben studies biology in college. His adviser tells him to decide what courses he will take and how much time he can allocate for the field research as a freshman. That, he says, increases the probability that he will get an assistant position as a senior.

A. Ben's adviser tells him to take as many courses as possible as a freshman.
B. Ben would likely have more opportunity to be an assistant later if he led a lot of outdoor activities.

訳

Ben は大学で生物学を勉強している。彼の担当教官は1回生の時にどの講義を取り、どれくらいの時間を野外研究に充てられるかを決めるよう Ben に言っている。担当教官が言うには、それが4回生になってから助手になれる可能性を大きくするらしい。

A. Ben の担当教官は彼に、できるだけ多くの講義を1回生の時に取るように言っている。

B. Ben は野外活動をたくさんおこなえば、あとで助手になる機会が多くなるようだ。

UNIT 3 試験形式の リスニング問題

▶UNIT 3の目標と問題形式

UNIT 1で英語音声の特徴を学び、UNIT 2で内容（コンテンツ）の聞き取りの練習をしました。UNIT 1とUNIT 2だけでもリスニング力は強化されますが、UNIT 3ではUNIT 1、UNIT 2の成果を英語資格試験形式の実践で使ってみましょう。

UNIT 3では、Part 1「選択肢だけ提示されたリスニング問題」とPart 2「Questionと選択肢が提示されたリスニング問題」に分けてチャレンジしてもらいます。「選択肢だけ提示された問題」とは、英検のようにQuestionは音声だけ流れて、Questionに対する解答の選択肢が問題用紙に提示されている形式です。
「Questionと選択肢が提示された問題」とは、TOEIC Listening & Reading Part 3、4のようにQuestionと選択枝の両方が提示されている問題です。

「選択肢だけ提示された問題」は英検やTEAP、TOEFL ITPなどで採用されていて、「Questionと選択肢が提示された問題」は、TOEIC、IELTSなどの試験に含まれています。

Part 1、Part 2ともに、〈1. ダイアローグ編（会話）〉と〈2. モノローグ編（話者一人）〉に分かれます。
Part 1はひとつの会話やモノローグに対してひとつの質問、Part 2はひとつの会話やモノローグに対して3つの質問に答えます。
レベルは英検2級、TOEIC L & R 400〜600点レベルの受験者を中心に想定しています。
「はじめに」で述べたように、Unit 1、2の表現がUnit 3で使われています。
解答ページの和訳の下にある 参照 は、センテンスや表現が使われているページを指します。

選択肢だけ提示されたリスニング問題

問題形式

「選択肢だけ提示されたリスニング問題」は、選択肢を見てリスニングの内容を推測します。例題を出します。英検2級第1部形式です。2者の会話に対する質問です。次の1〜4の選択肢が提示されています。

【選択肢】

1. He wants the newest models of earrings and necklaces.
2. He wants two different jewels if possible.
3. He wants the woman to buy both the necklace and earrings.
4. He is looking for an inexpensive diamond ring.

【訳】

1. 彼は最新モデルのイアリングとネックレスがほしい。
2. 彼は可能ならふたつの、違う宝石がほしい。
3. 彼はその女性にネックレスとイアリング両方買ってもらいたい。
4. 彼は高価でないダイアモンドの指輪を探している。

選択肢1〜4から何が推測できますか？

---

① 主語はすべて He なので、会話の中の男性のことだと推測できる。

② 4つの選択肢の necklace や earrings などから宝石の話だと推測できる。

では、その推測に沿って問題文（Track 30）を聞きます。まずはスクリプトを見ないで答えを出してみましょう。

皆さん、できましたか？　答えは2です。では、スクリプトを見ながら、もう一度聞いてみましょう。

🔊 **Track 30**

Sample Question

Woman: [3.] May I help you, sir?

Man: [4.] Yes, I'm looking for a necklace or a ring for my wife's birthday.
Could I look at the necklace on your right – the gold chain with a diamond pendant?

Woman: Certainly, sir. This is [1.] the newest design in our line this year. [2.] We have charming earrings that would go well with this chain, sir.

Man: [2.] Umm, I'd really like to get the earrings too. But I'd better check if those are within my budget.

Question: What is one thing that we can learn about the man?

訳：

Woman: いらっしゃいませ。

Man: 妻の誕生日プレゼントのネックレスか指輪を探しています。あなたの右側にあるネックレスを見せてもらえますか？ダイアモンドペンダントがついたゴールドチェーンのものです。

Woman: 承知しました。今年の品揃えの中で最新のデザインです。このチェーンに合うチャーミングなイアリングもあります。

Man: うーん、イアリングもいいですね。でも予算と相談してみないとね。

Question: この男性についてわかることのひとつは何ですか？

解答のポイント

Question を聞かなくても問題文の内容と合った選択肢はひとつしかありません。問題文を聞きながら記憶が新しいうちにマークを入れます。例題の選択肢をひとつずつ見ましょう。

1. He wants the newest models of earrings and necklaces.
2. He wants two different jewels if possible.
3. He wants the woman to buy both the necklace and earrings.
4. He is looking for an inexpensive diamond ring.

選択肢の　　　　部分がリスニングの内容と違った部分で、　　　　が内容と合っている部分です。

選択肢1
問題文で女性が the newest design（＿＿下線1）と言っているが男性は the newest model が欲しいとは言っていない。

選択肢2＝正解
問題文＿＿下線2で男性がネックレス以外に、女性が勧めたイアリングが予算内であれば買いたいと言っている。選択肢では問題文の chain や earrings ではなく two different jewels と言い換えている。

選択肢3
男性が客で女性が店員なので、男性が女性に何かを買ってほしいというのは内容と矛盾する。（＿＿下線3）

選択肢4

男性は diamond pendant がついた gold chain のネックレスが欲しい。ダイアモンドの指輪（diamond ring）を買うとは言っていない。（＿＿下線4）

皆さん、Question が出る前に解答できることが理解できましたか？ポイントをまとめます。

---

① 問題文を聞きながら答えをマークする

この例題の Question は「選択肢の中から事実を探しなさい」と同じ意味です。4つの選択肢に事実はひとつだけです。つまり、Question を聞く前に正解の選択肢を選ぶことができます。Question を聞いた後では記憶があいまいになりがちで誤答が多くなります（英検1級や TOEFL など、レベルが高くなると Question を聞かないと答えられない問題も出ますが、まずはこの方法をマスターしましょう）。

② 聞こえた単語だけで判断しない

会話に出てくる earrings、necklace、diamond、ring が入った1、3、4が正解ではありません。記憶があいまいになっていくと問題文に出た単語の記憶だけで選択肢を選びやすくなります。

③ 言い換えに注意

会話中の earrings と necklace が、正解の選択肢では two different jewels（ふたつの違った宝石）と言い換えられています。

④「ひっかけ」に注意。選択肢を理解する

3. He wants the woman to buy both the necklace and

earrings.（彼は女性にネックレスとイアリングを両方買って
ほしい）は the woman を省けば、つまり、He wants to buy
both the necklace and earrings.（彼はネックレスとイアリ
ング両方買いたい）なら正解。

解答のポイントを意識して問題にトライしましょう。ダイアローグ10問
とモノローグ10問です。選択肢だけが示されているので、音声を聞いて
正しい選択肢を選んでください。解答とスクリプトはダイアローグ編、モ
ノローグ編ともに問題の後にあります。

1. 選択肢だけ提示されたリスニング問題：ダイアローグ編

会話を聞いて、答えをひとつ選んでください。会話と問題のスクリプトは
提示されません。

Question 1 🔊 Track 31

1. She studied Chinese culture in college.
2. She went to a language school in summer.
3. She encouraged the man to travel around China.
4. She had Chinese classmates from all around China.

(Answer:)

Question 2 🔊 Track 32

1. He may not go out with the woman.
2. He doesn't want his client to pressure him.
3. He will get the okay from his superiors.
4. He visited Mellissa Corporation with the woman.

(Answer:)

Question 3 🔊 Track 33

1. Ask his mom about the official languages of Canada
2. Go to the library to read some books about Canadian history
3. Wait for his father to come home
4. Do his assignment right away

(Answer:　）

Question 4 🔊 Track 34

1. Order beef and fish dishes
2. Cook a fish dish
3. Decide her order
4. Serve smoked salmon

(Answer:　）

Question 5 🔊 Track 35

1. She lost her student ID card with a photo.
2. She can't get a library card.
3. She can't get her membership number.
4. She may not be able to check out books today.

(Answer:　）

Question 6 🔊 Track 36

1. Because she is 130 centimeters tall.
2. Because she can't get thrilled.
3. Because she loves Tornado Coaster.
4. Because she is shorter than the height limit.

(Answer:　）

Question 7 🔊 Track 37

1. She doesn't like the beach or the barbecue.
2. She will be taught how to make bread from an experienced baker.
3. She was asked to do so by the man.
4. She has to help her aunt run her shop.

(Answer:　)

Question 8 🔊 Track 38

1. He wanted the woman to turn off her mobile phone.
2. He should sharpen the edge of a knife.
3. He is in a rush to see his brother.
4. He is going to see someone on business.

(Answer:　)

Question 9 🔊 Track 39

1. He got a job because he had got a physical exam.
2. He was asked to see a doctor by his employer.
3. He is working hard at a trading company.
4. He will take a math exam today.

(Answer:　)

Question 10 🔊 Track 40

1. He works for a supermarket.
2. He will buy flour, sugar and butter to make cookies.
3. He is working in aisle 10.
4. He will show her some cookies to buy for her kids.

(Answer:　)

＊下線部が解答のヒントになる部分です。選択肢の　　　　部分の表現に気
を付けましょう。不正解のキーワードです。

Question 1　解答：2

スクリプト

Man: Hi, Jane. I heard you are studying Chinese. What made
you choose that difficult language?

Woman: Actually, I'd been interested in Asian cultures, so I joined
an intensive summer program when I found an ad of a
Chinese language school.

Man: I wish I could speak Chinese. I'd like to get a job at an
international enterprise after graduation.

Woman: Besides learning Chinese, it was fun meeting classmates
from all over the world. Some of them had traveled around
China many times.

Question: What can we learn about the woman?

1. She studied Chinese culture in college.
2. She went to a language school in summer.
3. She encouraged the man to travel around China.
4. She had Chinese classmates from all around China.

訳

Man: やあ、Jane。君が中国語を勉強しているって聞いたけど。な
ぜそんな難しい言語を選んだの？

Woman: 実はアジアの文化にずっと興味があって、だから中国語の語学

学校の広告を見つけて夏の集中講座に参加したの。

Man: ぼくも中国語が話せたらいいな。卒業したら国際企業に就職したいんだ。

Woman: 中国語を習うだけじゃなくて、世界中から来たクラスメートに合うことも楽しかった。その中には中国をあちこち何度も旅行した人もいたわ。

Question: 女性について何を知ることができますか？

1. 彼女は大学で中国文化を勉強した。
2. 彼女は夏に語学学校へ行った。
3. 彼女は男性に中国を旅することを勧めた。
4. 彼女には中国全土から来た中国人のクラスメートがいた。

 ボキャブラリー intensive 集中的な

参照 p. 36

Question 2　解答：1

スクリプト

Woman: What are you doing this afternoon? If you are free, would you come with me to Mellissa Corporation?

Man: Well, I'm waiting for a call from the client I told you about yesterday. She said she would get the okay from her superiors and call me in the morning.

Woman: It's already eleven thirty. I think you should give her a ring first thing after lunch.

Man: I would. But I wonder if she would feel I was pressuring her if I asked her to decide quickly.

Question: What can we infer about the man?

1. He may not go out with the woman.

2. He doesn't want his client to pressure him.

3. He will get the okay from his superiors.

4. He visited Mellissa Corporation with the woman.

訳

Woman: 午後の予定は？特になければ一緒に Mellissa Corporation に
行かない？

Man: そうですね。昨日お話したクライアントの電話を待っているん
ですよ。上司のオーケーを取って、午前中に電話すると言って
いたんですが。

Woman: もう11時半よ。昼食後すぐに電話した方がいいと思うわ。

Man: そうですね。でも、早く決断するようにお願いしたらプレッシ
ャーをかけていると思われないでしょうか。

Question: 男性について何が推測できますか？

1. 女性と一緒に出掛けないだろう。

2. クライアントにプレッシャーをかけられたくない。

3. 上司からオーケーを取るつもりだ。

4. 女性と Mellissa Corporation を訪ねた。

ボキャブラリー superior 上司　give a ring 電話をする

参照 p. 53、p. 58、p. 67、p. 75

Question 3　解答：3

スクリプト

Mom: Have you done your assignment, Ben? You said you
would research why Canada has two official languages.

Boy: Not yet, Mom. I think something's gone wrong with my
computer. I can't get online.

Mom: The Internet isn't the only source, I think. You could find some books about Canadian history in the library.

Boy: I wish I could, Mom. <u>The library is closed after five on Sundays.</u> I think Dad will be a life saver.

Question: What will Ben do?
1. Ask his mom about the official languages of Canada
2. Go to the library to read some books about Canadian history
3. Wait for his father to come home
4. Do his assignment right away

訳

Mom: 宿題はやったの、Ben? カナダにふたつの公用語がある理由を探すって言っていたでしょ。

Boy: まだだよ、お母さん。コンピューターがおかしいんだ。ネットにつながらないんだ。

Mom: インターネットだけが情報源じゃないでしょ。図書館でカナダ史の本を探せると思うわよ。

Boy: そうできればいいけど。<u>図書館は、日曜日5時以降は閉まっているんだ。</u>お父さんが助けてくれると思うよ。

Question: Ben はどうするつもりですか？
1. お母さんにカナダの公用語について質問する。
2. カナダ史の本を読むために図書館に行く。
3. お父さんが帰ってくるのを待つ。
4. すぐ宿題をやる。

ボキャブラリー assignment 宿題

参照 p. 26

Question 4　解答：3

スクリプト

Man: May I take your order? Today's recommendation is Kobe-beef with gravy.

Woman: Sounds great. But I'd rather have some fish. Do you have any codfish dishes?

Man: I'm sorry, we don't. We have grilled sole and smoked salmon. I recommend our onion salad with them.

Woman: OK. Could you give me a minute? I'll choose one of them.

Question: What will the woman do next?

1. Order beef and fish dishes
2. Cook a fish dish
3. Decide her order
4. Serve smoked salmon

訳

Man: ご注文はお決まりですか？本日のおすすめは神戸ビーフのグレービーソースがけでございます。

Woman: おいしそう。でも、さかながいいかしら。なにかタラ料理はある？

Man: 申し訳ございません。タラ料理はございません。舌平目の網焼きか、スモークサーモンならございます。一緒にオニオンサラダもおすすめです。

Woman: わかったわ。少し時間をいただける？どちらかを選ぶわ。

Question: 女性は次に何をするでしょう？

1. ビーフとさかな料理を注文する。
2. さかな料理を作る。
3. 注文を決める。
4. スモークサーモンを提供する。

Question 5　解答：4

スクリプト

Woman: I'd like to check out these books, but I think I've lost my library card.

Man: In that case, you need to apply for a new library card. Do you remember your membership number?

Woman: No, I don't. But I might have jotted it down. I can't get my card reissued without the number?

Man: No problem. If you have some photo ID, you can get a new one by tomorrow afternoon.

Question: What is the woman's problem?

1. She lost her student ID card with a photo.
2. She can't get a library card.
3. She can't get her membership number.
4. She may not be able to check out books today.

123

訳

Woman: これらの本を借り出したいんですが、図書カードを失くしたみたいなんです。

Man: その場合、新しい図書カードを申請する必要があります。会員番号を覚えていますか？

Woman: いいえ。でも、どこかに書いてあるかも。番号がなければ再発行できないんですか？

Man: できますよ。写真付きの身分証明証があれば、明日の午後には新しいカードをもらえます。

Question: 女性は何が問題ですか？

1. 彼女は写真付きの学生証を失くした。

2. 彼女は図書カードをもらえない。

3. 彼女は会員番号がもらえない。

4. 彼女は、今日本を借り出せないかもしれない。

ボキャブラリー reissue 再発行する

参照 p. 18、p. 58

Question 6　解答：4

スクリプト

Woman: I'd like to ride Thunder Mountain Coaster with my eight-year-old daughter. She loves to get thrilled by amusement park rides. Do you have an age limit?

Man: The lower age limit is seven years old. But we also have a height limit.

Woman: My daughter is 120 centimeters tall. Can she go on the ride?

Man: Sorry, ma'am. Anyone whose height is below 130 centimeters can't ride this attraction. We have Tornado Coaster in the North Area, though. Its height limit is 110 centimeters.

Question: Why can't the woman's daughter ride Thunder Mountain Coaster?

1. Because she is 130 centimeters tall.

2. Because she can't get thrilled.

3. Because she loves Tornado Coaster.

4. Because she is shorter than the height limit.

Woman: Thunder Mountain Coaster に8歳の娘と乗りたいんですが。アトラクションが大好きなんです。年齢制限はありますか?

Man: 年齢の下限は7歳ですが、身長制限もあります。

Woman: 娘は120 cm です。乗れますか?

Man: すみません。130 cm 以下の方はこのアトラクションに乗れません。北エリアに Tornado Coaster がありますよ。身長制限は110 cm です。

Question: なぜ女性の娘は Thunder Mountain Coaster に乗れないのでしょうか?

1. 130 cm だから。

2. ワクワクできないから。

3. Tornado Coaster が好きだから。

4. 身長制限より低いから。

125

ボキャブラリー　get thrilled ワクワクする　amusement park ride 遊園地のアトラクション

参照　p. 28、p. 70

Question 7　解答：4

スクリプト

Man: Do you have any plans for summer vacation, Karen?

Woman: No, Jasper. I'll just work at my aunt's bakery.

Man: No kidding! You'll work the whole summer? I didn't know you were such a workaholic. I can't live without the beach and the barbecue!!

Woman: Don't talk to me about the beach and barbecue!! I really want a vacation with my friends. But I have no choice. My aunt has no family and the most experienced baker just quit.

Question: Why is the woman going to stay home during summer?
1. She doesn't like the beach or the barbecue.
2. She will be taught how to make bread from an experienced baker.
3. She was asked to do so by the man.
4. She has to help her aunt run her shop.

訳

Man: Karen、夏休みの予定はなにかあるの？
Woman: ないわ、Jasper。おばさんのパン屋で働くだけ。
Man: 冗談はよせよ！夏の間ずっと働くって？君がそんな仕事中毒だとは知らなかったよ。ぼくはビーチとバーベキューなしでは生きていけないよ。
Woman: 私にビーチとかバーベキューとか言わないでよ!!友達とのバケーションが望みなんだから。でも、しかたないのよ。おばさんは家族がいないし、一番経験があるパン職人が辞めたばかりだから。

Question: なぜ女性は夏中ずっと家にいるのでしょう？
1. 彼女はビーチやバーベキューが好きでない。
2. 経験豊かなパン職人からパンの作り方を習う。
3. 男性にそうするように言われた。
4. おばさんが店を経営するのを助ける。

ボキャブラリー　workaholic　仕事中毒

Question 8　解答：4

スクリプト

Woman: Sir, could you please keep your smartphone turned off while the seatbelt sign is on?

Man: But we've already landed. <u>I need to call a client I'm meeting with today</u> – as soon as possible.

Woman: I understand you are in a hurry, but for safety, you need to observe our in-flight rules.

Man: All right. I'm sorry that I was on edge.

Question: What do we learn about the man?

1. He wanted the woman to turn off her mobile phone.
2. He should sharpen the edge of a knife.
3. He is in a rush to see his brother.
4. He is going to see someone on business.

訳

Woman: すみません。シートベルト着用サインが出ている間はスマートフォンの電源をお切り願えませんか？

Man: でも、もう着陸したでしょ。今日ミーティングするクライアントに、できるだけ早く電話しないといけないんです。

Woman: お急ぎのことはわかりますが、安全のために機内規則をお守りいただかないといけません。

Man: わかりました。イライラしてすみません。

Question: 男性について何がわかりますか？

1. 彼は女性に携帯電話の電源を切ってもらいたい。
2. 彼はナイフの刃を研がないといけない。
3. 彼は兄弟に会うために急いでいる。
4. 彼は仕事である人に会う予定だ。

ボキャブラリー   in-flight 機内の   sharpen the edge 刃を研ぐ

参照   p. 18、p. 29、p. 68

Question 9　解答：2

スクリプト

Woman: So, your chart says that you are here for your checkup.

Man: Yes, Doctor. <u>I just got a position at a trading company and they are requiring me to get a physical.</u>

Woman: When did you last come in for one? Have you felt any discomfort recently?

Man: I haven't been here for a while. I've been working hard to stay healthy. I hope the tests turn out well.

Question: What is one thing that is true about the man?

1. He got a job because he had got a physical exam.

2. He was asked to see a doctor by his employer.

3. He is working hard at a trading company.

4. He will take a math exam today.

訳

Woman: それで、カルテを見ると、健康診断で来られたんですね。

Man: はい、先生。貿易会社に就職したばかりなんですが、健康診断を受けるように言われているんです。

Woman: 前はいつ受けに来られました？最近具合の悪いところはありますか？

Man: 長い間来ていません。ずっと健康維持に努めていました。結果が良ければいいんですが。

Question: 男性について事実はどれですか？

1. 健康診断を受けたので、職を得た。

128

2. 雇用主に医者に行くように言われた。

3. 貿易会社で一生懸命働いている。

4. 今日、数学のテストを受ける。

Question 10　解答：1

スクリプト

Man: Can I help you find something ma'am?

Woman: Yes, I want to bake some cookies for my kids. The recipe calls for flour, sugar and butter.

Man: Those ingredients are in aisle 10. Let me show you where they are.

Woman: Oh, and I also need eggs and chocolate chips.

129

Question: What do we learn about the man?

1. He works for a supermarket.

2. He will buy flour, sugar and butter to make cookies.

3. He is working in aisle 10.

4. He will show her some cookies to buy for her kids.

訳

Man: 何かお探しですか？

Woman: はい。子供たちにクッキーを焼いてあげたいんです。レシピには小麦粉、砂糖、バターが要ると書いてあります。

Man: それらの食材は10番通路にあります。ご案内します。

Woman: そうだ、卵とチョコチップも必要です。

Question: 男性について何がわかりますか？
1. 彼はスーパーマーケットで働いている。
2. 彼はクッキーを作るために小麦粉、砂糖、バターを買う。
3. 彼は10番通路で働いている。
4. 彼は彼女に、子供たちに買うためのクッキーを見せる。

ボキャブラリー call for 必要とする

2. 選択肢だけ提示されたリスニング問題：モノローグ編

音声を聞いて問題の答えとなる選択肢をひとつ選んでください。

Question 1　◁)) Track 41

1. He suffered under slavery after he had become a politician.
2. He became a member of the U.S. Congress after he had been freed.
3. He wrote several books about other statesmen.
4. He was a leader of slaves in Maryland.

(Answer:　　)

Question 2　◁)) Track 42

1. He wants to be a government employee specializing in international relations.
2. He is working part-time in a country where English is spoken.
3. He wants to improve his language ability by going abroad.
4. His English grade is poor because he is working part-time.

(Answer:　　)

Question 3　◁)) Track 43

1. Keep from reclining their seats
2. Welcome passengers
3. Turn on the seatbelt sign for their safety
4. Keep their seatbelts and seats at hand

(Answer:　　)

Question 4 🔊 Track 44

1. Each hand moves differently to play this instrument.
2. Street musicians are engaged in selling barrel organs.
3. The audience needs to press keys to help the player.
4. It originated in Asia and later was exported to Europe.

(Answer:　)

Question 5 🔊 Track 45

1. He usually checks to see if his data is backed up while driving his car.
2. It took him 90 days to get an International Driving Permit.
3. He has to take into consideration a traffic jam on his way to the office.
4. He has visited some cities which have the longest commuting times.

(Answer:　)

Question 6 🔊 Track 46

1. Their vehicles caught on fire because of faulty electric wiring.
2. Some of them got involved in an accident on the UG Highway.
3. They had to take different routes on which the traffic was heavy.
4. Their office was closed five hours after the accident.

(Answer:　)

Question 7 🔊 Track 47

1. He teaches some students for the doctoral degree.
2. His wife's family run in a sports festival.
3. He fries potatoes for a restaurant in London.
4. He takes days off for his family a couple of times a year.

(Answer:　)

Question 8 🔊 Track 48

1. To work longer hours
2. To work full-time though she should sometimes go back home early
3. To be absent from work, because she is a part-timer
4. To study the flex time system after her working hours

(Answer:　)

Question 9 🔊 Track 49

1. It has been extinct for more than 20 years.
2. It is kept as a pet by some Native American tribes.
3. It has survived the 20th century.
4. It eats meat and vegetables.

(Answer:　)

133

Question 10 🔊 Track 50

1. They aggressively speak to their passengers.
2. They buy inexpensive cars to drive around in.
3. They may make their passengers pay a lot.
4. They might be tricked to pay some extra money.

(Answer:　)

解答

＊下線部が解答のヒントになる部分です。選択肢の ▢▢▢ 部分の表現に気を付けましょう。不正解のキーワードです。

Question 1　解答：2
スクリプト

Frederick Douglass is one of the most eminent African Americans in American history. He was born a slave in 1818 in Maryland. He escaped from slavery and later became a statesman. He was a leader of the U.S. abolitionist movement – a nationwide campaign to free slaves. He was not only an influential politician but also the owner of a newspaper company. He himself was an author of several books based on his life story.

Question: What can we infer about Frederick Douglass?

1. He suffered under slavery after he had become a politician.
2. He became a member of the U.S. Congress after he had been freed.
3. He wrote several books about other statesmen.
4. He was a leader of slaves in Maryland.

訳

Frederick Douglass はアメリカの歴史の中で最も著名なアフリカ系アメリカ人の一人だ。彼は1818年、Maryland で奴隷として生まれた。彼は奴隷の状態から逃げ出し、後に政治家になった。彼はアメリカの abolitionist 運動 —奴隷解放の全国的な運動— のリーダーの一人だった。彼は影響力

134

がある政治家だったばかりでなく、新聞社のオーナーでもあった。彼自身も自伝的な本の著者でもあった。

Question: Frederick Douglass に関して何が推測できますか？
    1. 彼は政治家になった後に奴隷として苦しんだ。
    2. 彼は奴隷から解放された後に国会のメンバーになった。
    3. 彼は自分以外の政治家について何冊かの本を書いた。
    4. 彼は Maryland で奴隷のリーダーだった。

ボキャブラリー eminent 著名な　abolitionist movement 奴隷解放運動
参照 p. 28、p. 30

Question 2　解答：3
スクリプト

Keisuke is a college student who majors in international relations. He is interested in studying in a country where English is its official language, because he is thinking about working for an international corporation after graduation. He is working part-time to save money to go to a college abroad. He believes that working part-time will help him improve his communication ability as well.

Question: What is one thing we learn about Keisuke?
    1. He wants to be a government employee specializing in international relations.
    2. He is working part-time in a country where English is spoken.
    3. He wants to improve his language ability by going abroad.
    4. His English grade is poor because he is working part-time.

訳
圭介は国際関係を専攻する大学生だ。彼は英語が公用語の国で勉強することに興味がある。なぜなら、彼は卒業後国際企業で働こうと思っているからだ。彼は海外の大学に行くためにアルバイトをしてお金を貯めている。彼は、アルバイトが自分のコミュニケーション能力上達の助けにもなると信じている。

Question: 圭介について何を知ることができますか？
    1. 彼は国際関係専門の政府職員になりたい。
    2. 彼は英語が話されている国でアルバイトをしている。
    3. 彼は海外へ行くことで語学力を伸ばしたい。
    4. 彼はアルバイトをしているので英語の成績が悪い。

参照　p. 28、p. 58、p. 68

Question 3　解答：1
スクリプト

Good morning, passengers. Welcome aboard Elegant Airline Flight 101 for London. The captain of this flight is George Marcus, and my co-pilot is Taro Kobayashi. We will be taking off in a minute. Please be sure to fasten your seat belt and keep your seat in its original position while the seatbelt sign is on.

Question: What is one thing that the listeners should do?
    1. Keep from reclining their seats
    2. Welcome passengers
    3. Turn on the seatbelt sign for their safety
    4. Keep their seatbelts and seats at hand

皆様、おはようございます。ELEGANT エアライン 101 便ロンドン行きにご搭乗いただきありがとうございます。本機の機長は George Marcus、副機長は小林太郎です。当機は間もなく離陸いたします。<u>シートベルト着用サインが点灯している間はシートベルトをお締めになり、シートを元の位置にお戻しいただくようお願い申し上げます。</u>

Question: このアナウンスを聞いている人がすべきことのひとつは何ですか？

    1. シートをリクライニングしない。

    2. 乗客を迎える。

    3. 安全のためにシートベルト着用サインを点灯させる。

    4. シートベルトとシートを手元に置く。

参照 p. 39

Question 4　解答：1

Kaori first saw a hurdy-gurdy played while traveling around Spain. It was being played by a street musician on the street in Madrid. The hurdy-gurdy is a stringed musical instrument that originated in Europe. <u>This instrument is played by turning a handle with one hand and pressing keys with the other.</u> It is also called a "barrel organ" or "street piano".

Question: What is one thing that we learn about the hurdy-gurdy?

    1. Each hand moves differently to play this instrument.

    2. Street musicians are engaged in selling barrel organs.

    3. The audience needs to press keys to help the player.

    4. It originated in Asia and later was exported to Europe.

訳

佳織はスペインを旅行中に初めてハーディー・ガーディーが演奏されているのを見た。それは Madrid の街頭でストリートミュージシャンによって演奏されていた。ハーディー・ガーディーはヨーロッパ発祥の弦楽器である。この楽器は片手でハンドルを回し、もう片方の手で鍵盤を押すことで演奏される。これはバレルオルガンやストリートピアノと呼ばれることもある。

Question: ハーディー・ガーディーについて何を知ることができますか？

  1. この楽器を演奏するためには両手が違う動きをする。
  2. ストリートミュージシャンたちはバレルオルガンの販売に携わっている。
  3. 聴衆は奏者を助けるために鍵盤を押す必要がある。
  4. この楽器はアジア発祥で、後にヨーロッパへ輸出された。

138

参照 p. 40、p. 59、p. 60

Question 5　解答：3

スクリプト

When Mr. Yamada was transferred to Philadelphia, he got an International Driving Permit. He has found that it takes him more than 90 minutes to drive from his suburban home to his downtown office. Philadelphia is one of the cities that has the longest commuting times in the United States. He has to leave really early, for fear of getting caught in backups along the way.

Question: What can be inferred about Mr. Yamada?

  1. He usually checks to see if his data is backed up while driving his car.
  2. It took him 90 days to get an International Driving

Permit.

3. He has to take into consideration a traffic jam on his way to the office.

4. He has visited some cities which have the longest commuting times.

訳

山田さんが Philadelphia に転勤になった時、彼は国際運転免許を取得した。彼の郊外の家から町の中心地にあるオフィスまでは車で90分以上かかることがわかった。Philadelphia はアメリカでもっとも通勤時間が長くかかる都市のひとつだ。彼は通勤で交通渋滞に巻き込まれることが怖いので、かなり早く家を出ないといけない。

Question: 山田さんについて何が推測できますか？

1. 彼は普段車を運転中に、データがバックアップされているかをチェックする。

2. 国際運転免許証を取得るのに90日かかった。

3. 彼はオフィスへ行く道の交通渋滞を計算に入れなければならない。

4. 彼は、通勤時間が最もかかるいくつかの都市を訪ねた。

ボキャブラリー backup 交通渋滞　back up（データなどを）バックアップする
参照 p. 40、p. 59

Question 6　解答：3

スクリプト

A heavy truck carrying tons of electric wires exploded into flames this morning. This disaster happened around five in the morning on Route 5. The road is still closed five hours after the explosion. It is the worst day for the commuters to Gold City. They have been forced to take Routes 1 and 3. There's been bumper-to-bumper traffic on Green Drive East near the UG Highway.

Question: What happened to the commuters?

1. Their vehicles caught on fire because of faulty electric wiring.
2. Some of them got involved in an accident on the UG Highway.
3. They had to take different routes on which the traffic was heavy.
4. Their office was closed five hours after the accident.

訳

今朝、数トンの電線を積んだ大型トラックが爆発し、炎上した。この災害はルート5で朝5時に発生した。この道は爆発の5時間後でもまだ閉鎖されている。Gold City への通勤者にとって最悪の日である。彼らはルート1とルート3を使わざるを得なくなっている。UG Highway 近くの Green Drive East では、大渋滞が起こっている。

Question: 通勤者たちに何が起こっていますか？

1. 誤った配線で彼らの車が燃えた。
2. 何人かが UG Highway の事故に巻き込まれた。
3. 彼らは交通量が多い、違ったルートを使わないといけなかった。
4. 彼らのオフィスは事故後5時間で閉まった。

ボキャブラリー catch on fire 燃える
参照 p. 19、p. 69

Question 7 解答：4

Thomas is from Canada, and is leading a busy life in Japan. He teaches English at several universities in Kyoto. During the summer, he flies to London for his doctoral studies. During the Golden Week vacation, he helps out at the traditional Japanese inn his wife's family runs. He cleans the big bath. <u>Although he spends such busy days, he makes it a rule to take vacations with his family in summer and the Christmas season.</u>

Question: What is one thing that we learn about Thomas?

    1. He teaches some students for the doctoral degree.

    2. His wife's family run in a sports festival.

    3. He fries potatoes for a restaurant in London.

    4. He takes days off for his family a couple of times a year.

Thomas はカナダ出身で、日本で忙しい日々を過ごしている。彼は京都のいくつかの大学で英語を教えている。彼は夏の間博士号取得のためロンドンに飛ぶ。ゴールデンウィークには、奥さんの家族が経営する伝統的な（日本式）旅館を手伝う。彼は大浴場の掃除担当だ。<u>彼はそんな忙しい日々を過ごしているが、夏とクリスマスの時期には家族と休暇を取ることにしている。</u>

Question: Thomas について何を知ることができますか？

    1. 彼は何人かの学生に博士号取得のための勉強を教えている。

    2. 彼の奥さんの家族は体育祭で走る。

    3. 彼はロンドンのレストランのためにポテトを揚げる。

    4. 彼は年に何回か家族のために休暇を取る。

参照 p. 19、p. 30、p. 56、p. 69

Question 8 解答：2

スクリプト

Keiko is a working mother with a baby boy. After taking maternity leave, she returned to work. She is now working part-time, because she sometimes has to either leave work earlier or be absent from work because her son, Toku, often has a fever. She wishes that more Japanese companies had flex-time for the benefit of female workers, especially, for working mothers like herself.

Question: What does Keiko most likely want?

1. To work longer hours
2. To work full-time though she should sometimes go back home early
3. To be absent from work, because she is a part-timer
4. To study the flex time system after her working hours

訳

圭子は男の子の赤ちゃんがいるワーキングマザーだ。彼女は育児休暇を取った後、仕事に復帰した。彼女はパートで働いている。なぜなら、しばしば息子である徳が熱を出すので早めに退社したり、会社を休んだりしないといけないからだ。彼女はより多くの日本の会社が女性従業員のために、特に彼女のようなワーキングマザーのために、フレックスタイムを導入していればいいなと思う。

Question: 圭子は何を最も望んでいる可能性がありますか？

1. より長時間働くこと。
2. 時々早く帰らないといけないが、正社員で働くこと。
3. 仕事を休むこと。パートタイマーだから。

4. 就業時間後にフレックスタイムについて学ぶこと。

ボキャブラリー maternity leave 育児休暇

参照 p. 31、p. 67

Question 9　解答：3

スクリプト

The California condor is the largest flying bird in North America. It is carnivorous, which means that it eats meat, not plants. This species almost became extinct in the 20th century. Continuous efforts have been made to save it. Thanks to a variety of preservation activities, its population has slightly increased. The California condor is also a sacred bird for some Native American tribes.

Question: What can we learn about the California condor?
　　　1. It has been extinct for more than 20 years.
　　　2. It is kept as a pet by some Native American tribes.
　　　3. It has survived the 20th century.
　　　4. It eats meat and vegetables.

訳

カリフォルニアコンドルは飛行する鳥では北米最大だ。彼らは肉食だ。すなわち、植物ではなく肉を食べる。この種は20世紀に絶滅しかけた。彼らを救うために継続的な努力がなされてきた。多様な保護活動のおかげで、その数は少し増えた。カリフォルニアコンドルはいくつかのネイティブアメリカンの部族にとって神聖な鳥でもある。

Question: カリフォルニアコンドルについて何がわかりますか？
　　　1. 絶滅して20年経つ。
　　　2. いくつかのネイティブアメリカンの部族にペットとして飼わ

れている。

3. 彼らは20世紀を生き延びた。

4. 彼らは肉と野菜を食べる。

ボキャブラリー　carnivorous 肉食の　sacred 神聖な　tribe 部族

参照　p. 28

Question 10　解答：3

スクリプト

Mr. Suzuki goes on a business trip to China and South Korea several times a year. He has found that taking taxis is an inexpensive way to get around in both countries. They are much cheaper than those in Japan, but the drivers, he feels, drive a little too aggressively. He may make a business trip to some other countries in the future. He heard that in some countries, there are taxi drivers who might trick the passengers into paying some extra money. He thinks he must be cautious when taking a cab abroad.

Question: What can be inferred about some taxi drivers?

　　　1. They aggressively speak to their passengers.

　　　2. They buy inexpensive cars to drive around in.

　　　3. They may make their passengers pay a lot.

　　　4. They might be tricked to pay some extra money.

訳

鈴木さんは年に数回中国と韓国に出張する。彼は、このふたつの国でタクシーが安価な移動手段あることが分かった。それらのタクシーは日本のタクシーよりかなり安いが、運転手は少し荒っぽいと感じる。彼は将来、他の国々へ出張するかも知れない。彼は、ある国では客をだましてお金を余分に払わせるタクシードライバーがいると聞いた。彼は海外でタクシーに

乗るときは気を付けなければと思う。

Question: あるタクシードライバーについて何が推測できますか？
    1. 彼らは乗客に荒っぽく話す。
    2. 彼らは移動するために安い車を買う。
    3. 彼らは客に高い料金を払わせる時がある。
    4. 彼らはだまされて高い料金を払うことがある。

ボキャブラリー trick 〜 into … 〜をだまして…させる
参照 p. 13

Part 2

問題と選択肢が提示されたリスニング問題

問題形式

Part 1 はうまくできましたか？ Part 2 では選択肢だけでなく問題も示されているリスニング問題にチャレンジしてもらいます。でも、選択肢だけが示されている問題よりも簡単だと考えてはだめですよ。

まず、問題数が多くなる傾向があります。Part 1 「選択肢だけが提示されたリスニング問題」は英検 2 級タイプの問題で、ダイアローグやモノローグひとつに対して問題がひとつでしたが、「問題と選択肢が提示されたリスニング問題」はひとつのダイアローグやモノローグに対して、問題が 3 つ以上出題されることが多いのです。

この形式でも Part 1 と同じように先読みが鍵になります。例を出しましょう。TOEIC Listening & Reading Part 3 の形式です。Question 1〜3 に各々4つ、A〜D の選択肢があります。Questions と選択肢を読んで会話の内容を推測してみましょう。

Sample Questions 1 to 3

1. Who most likely are the speakers?
   - A. Colleagues
   - B. Professor Singh's friends
   - C. Students
   - D. Dental patients

2. What does Professor Singh do for her students?
   - A. Access some websites to listen to recorded lectures

B. Put audio files online

C. Download her own lectures

D. Show them her notes if they have trouble following her lectures

3. What does the woman advise the man to do?

A. To record their conversation

B. To go to the dentist

C. To see her notes

D. To visit a website

【訳】

1. 誰が話している可能性が一番高いですか？

A. 同僚

B. Singh 教授の友人

C. 学生

D. 歯科の患者

2. Singh 教授は学生達のために何をしていますか？

A. 録音された講義を聴くためにウェブサイトにアクセスする

B. 音声記録をネットに載せる

C. 自分の講義をダウンロードする

D. 学生達がついて来られないときは自分のノートを見せる

3. 女性は男性に何をするようにアドバイスしていますか？

A. 自分たちの会話を録音すること。

B. 歯医者に行くこと

C. 彼女のノートを見ること

D. ウェブサイトを見る（訪れる）こと

どれくらい内容を推測できましたか？もちろん正確な内容は推測できません。ある程度予測して、ダイアローグを聞きながら答えを出していきます。聞き終わってからでは遅いのです。では、Question の順で見ていきましょう。

Question 1

選択肢Ａ〜Ｄから、どんな人の会話なのかある程度推測できます。Colleagues（同僚）なら取引の話などのビジネス関係の会話だろうし、Students（学生）なら勉強や試験などの話かもしれないと推測します。Professor Singh's friends（Singh 教授の友人）で、会話の中に Professor Singh という人が登場することが推測されます。Dental patients（歯科の患者）で会話の中に Dentist に関連した内容が含まれる可能性を推測します。

Question 2

Question から Singh 教授が学生たちのために何かをしていることがわかります。website や access, download などで、インターネットが関連していることを推測します。

Question 3

問題文から女性が男性に何かアドバイスしていることが推測できます。選択肢から「記録、録音する」「歯医者」、「インターネット」「ノート」などの内容が含まれることが推測できます。

この形式のリスニングは Question の順番に沿って会話の内容が展開されることがほとんどです。最初の問題のヒントが最後にあって、最後の問題のヒントが最初に来ることは基本的にありません。
まず、Question 1 に集中します。会話の前半に答えがあります。Question 1 の答えが出たら、すぐに Question 2 の選択肢を見ながら会話に集中します。2 の答えが出たら 3 へと進みます。

では、ここまでの推測を元に会話（Track 51）を聞きながら、スクリプトは見ないで、Questions の答えを出してみましょう。まだこの問題形式に慣れていない場合は、音声をセンテンス単位で止めながら、その時点で解答できるかを確認しながら進めるのも良いでしょう。会話の流れに沿ったQuestions の答え方が理解できるかもしれません。

🔊 **Track 51**

どうでしょうか？答えがでましたか？

解答は　1. C　2. B　3. D です。

解答のポイント

ではスクリプトを見ながらもう一度聞いて確認しましょう。

🔊 **Track 51**

Sample Questions 1 to 3

Man: [1.] Did you go to today's Economics 101 class?

Woman: Yup. Didn't see you there.

Man: Had a dental appointment. Did you take notes?

Woman: I did. [2.] But Professor Singh records her lectures. You can download them and listen to any you missed.

Man: Awesome! Okay. Where can I access them?

Woman: [3.] Well, first, go to her web page. It's really easy to find them.

Man: Okay. I'll do that. If I have trouble following it, can I still see your notes?

Woman: No sweat.

(ボキャブラリー)　No sweat お安いご用、朝飯前、へいっちゃら

【訳】

Man: [1.] 今日の Economics 101 の授業出た？

Woman: うん。あなた、見かけなかったね。

Man: 歯医者の予約があったんだ。ノート取った？

Woman: ええ。²·でも Singh 教授は自分の講義を録音しているのよ。出られなかった講義をダウンロードして聴けるの。

Man: そりゃすごい！どうやってアクセスできるんだい？

Woman: ³·先生のウェブページに行けば、録音した講義は簡単に見つかるわ。

Man: わかった。やってみる。内容について行けなかったらノートを見せてくれる？

Woman: お安いご用よ。

では、スクリプトに沿って問題別に解答を確認しましょう。下線部が答えのヒントになる部分です。下線部の先頭に1～3の番号がふってあるので、Question ナンバー別に確認してください。

Question 1

最初の Economics 101 class（経済学101クラス）で大学での会話だとわかるので、Question 1の解答は C. Students になります。

Question 2

But Professor Singh records her lectures. You can download them and listen to any you missed.（でも Singh 教授は自分の講義を録音しているのよ。出られなかった講義をダウンロードして聴けるの。）から、Singh 教授が自分の講義を録音して、ダウンロードできるようにしていることがわかるので、2の解答を B. Put audio files online（音声記録をネットに載せる）にします。

Question 3

Well, first, go to her web page. を言い換えた D が答えになります。ダイアローグでは her web page（彼女のウェブページ）で Singh 教授のウェブページと特定していますが、選択肢では a website（あるウェブサイト）で、あいまいな表現にしています。Part 1 と同じく正解の選択肢

に含まれる選択肢は言い換えられたり、あいまいな表現になることが多いのです。

ここで説明したように、Question 1～3をリスニングしながら順に答えていきます。聞き終わってからでは遅いのです。では、問題にチャレンジしましょう。

TOEIC は級別に難易度が分かれていません。ビジネスで使う表現も多いので Part 1 の問題よりも難しく感じるかもしれませんが、練習なのでトライしましょう。Part 1 と同じくダイアローグ（会話）が10題、モノローグ（話者一人）が10題で1題に Question が3つです。

1. 問題と選択肢が提示されたリスニング問題：ダイアローグ編

Questions 1 – 3 ◁» Track 52

1. What does the woman infer about the man?

   A. He is shipping a client's order.

   B. He is wiping his desk all morning long.

   C. He has to talk to Daniel in R & D.

   D. He has gone out with his coworker.

   (Answer:)

2. What does the man mean when he says, "I'm proud of my work 'n' all I've done since I came here. But...."?

   A. He doesn't feel satisfied with his performance.

   B. He regrets that he hung around with his colleague.

   C. He wants the woman to earn double.

   D He feels he should be paid as much as his colleague.

   (Answer:)

3. What is the man planning to do?

    A. Have a talk at Moon Mart

    B. Present his idea to the woman

    C. Go ahead with his marketing research

    D. Talk about MP3 SUPER

(Answer:)

Questions 4 – 6　◁)) Track 53

4. What is the man's problem?

    A. He has trouble with the Thompson account.

    B. He has a private matter to attend to during his work hours.

    C. He missed one of his afternoon assignments.

    D. He must introduce Ms. Anderson to the Thompsons

(Answer:)

5. What can be inferred about the man's sister?

    A. She lives with the man.

    B. She is single.

    C. She sees the man every Thursday.

    D. She has one or more children.

(Answer:)

6. What does the woman say about sick leave?

    A. The man can get sick leave for one year.

    B. Sick leave can be taken only in June.

    C. Payment is not made for the first year.

    D. June is the first month the employees can get sick leave.

(Answer:)

7. What is the woman's problem?

    A. The blouse is too small for her.

    B. She lost the receipt for the pants and the jacket.

    C. She feels none of her clothes go well with the blouse she bought.

    D. The shop doesn't have any pants or jackets to her taste.

                              （Answer: ）

8. What is the reason the woman can't exchange the item?

    A. She isn't sure when she bought it.

    B. She got the item too long ago.

    C. She has exchanged the item before.

    D. The blouse was a good bargain on July 5th.

                              （Answer: ）

153

9. What is one thing the man offers the woman?

    A. Some wrapping

    B. A coupon

    C. A replacement

    D. A defective item

                              （Answer: ）

10. What is the problem?

    A. Susan has complaints about their telephone support.

    B. The technical representatives repeat the same complaints.

    C. Their support line is short-staffed.

    D. They can't reach their customers on their website.

                              （Answer: ）

11. Why does Greg think they should outsource their support line?

    A. Because it's cost-effective.

    B. Because it will double the customers.

    C. Because he can gain some degree of expertise.

    D. Because it is called "the graveyard shift."

(Answer:　)

12. What does Jake say about outsourcing their support line?

    A. Foreign staff may not like American users.

    B. They will research it.

    C. He doubts the expertise of the support center staff.

    D. Foreign staff have enough communication skills.

(Answer:　)

Questions 13 – 15 ◁))) **Track 56**

13. Where is this conversation probably taking place?

    A. At a family home

    B. At a church

    C. At an office

    D. At a warehouse

(Answer:　)

14. What is the woman's concern?

    A. Losing an advantage over their rivals

    B. Becoming less edgy

    C. Taking the edge off

    D. Their competitive nature

(Answer:　)

15. What is the man's concern?

    A. The competition

    B. The upstairs neighbor

    C. The effectiveness of the latest OS

    D. The expenses

                                                （Answer: ）

Questions 16 – 18 （Three speakers） 🔊 **Track 57**

16. Where is this conversation most likely taking place?

    A. A financial institution in Canada

    B. A bank in the U.S.

    C. An exchange counter in Japan

    D. A trading company

                                                （Answer: ）

17. What most likely is the reason the woman says, "Really? I thought the exchange rate was about 102 yen to the dollar"?

    A. Canada and the U.S. are similar countries.

    B. The rates of two currencies are similar.

    C. The names of two currencies are similar.

    D. They're communicating online.

                                                （Answer: ）

18. What is true about the American dollar?

    A. It is more valuable than the Canadian currency.

    B. It is about the same value as the Canadian currency.

    C. It is less valuable than the Canadian currency.

    D. Its value fluctuates.

                                                （Answer: ）

19. Where is this conversation most likely taking place?

    A. On the phone

    B. At the travel agency

    C. By instant message

    D. By email

    （Answer:　 ）

20. What can we infer about the woman?

    A. She has people who can show her around London and Paris.

    B. She is a bargain hunter.

    C. She speaks French.

    D. She loves cable TV channels.

    （Answer:　 ）

156

21. What does the woman request of the man?

    A. To join a guided tour

    B. To take a tour of the Channel

    C. To contact her later

    D. To e-mail her during Easter

    （Answer:　 ）

Questions 22 – 24　（Three speakers）　🔊 **Track 59**

22. Who is most likely the woman?

    A. A salesclerk

    B. The sales manager

    C. The company president

    D. A manufacturer

    （Answer:　 ）

23. What can we infer about the woman?

    A. She is very prepared.

    B. She needs to listen to her subordinates' suggestions.

    C. She is not as prepared as she could be.

    D. She is more prepared than she needs to be.

                                             (Answer:)

24. What will probably be discussed at the next meeting?

    A. Why sales fall so dramatically in August and how to provide better service

    B. Why sales fall so dramatically in July and how to provide better service

    C. Why sales fall so dramatically in August and how to understand the customers better

    D. When to put fall clothes on display

                                             (Answer:)

157

Questions 25 – 27 ◁») **Track 60**

25. What can we infer about the guests?

    A. They do not eat mayonnaise.

    B. They are not vegetarians.

    C. They are allergic to dairy products.

    D. They are on a diet.

                                             (Answer:)

26. What can be inferred about the speakers?

    A. They will be serving alcohol.

    B. They will be serving tea.

    C. They won't be serving their guests anything to drink.

    D. They won't be serving alcohol to their guests.

    (Answer:)

27. What, probably, is the situation?

    A. A couple is entertaining friends.

    B. Business associates are entertaining clients.

    C. Classmates are planning a study session.

    D. Parents are entertaining their children.

    (Answer:)

Questions 28 – 30 🔊 **Track 61**

28. Why is the restaurant full now?

    A. Because twenty parties are held at the same time.

    B. Because they are celebrating their 20th anniversary.

    C. Because a large group is occupying many tables.

    D. Because regular staff are not available today.

    (Answer:)

29. What does the man say about the special offers?

    A. They are for a limited time.

    B. They are for his fifth wedding anniversary.

    C. The restaurant serves different dinners every day.

    D. They are not on the menu.

    (Answer:)

30. Look at the menu. How much will each member of the woman's party pay?

Today's Menu

Set Menu A $40   **Set Menu B $45**

Appetizer

Marinated Tomato   Eggplant Pickles

Soup

Pescador Onion Soup   Spanish Garlic Soup

Salad

Burdock Salad   Caesar Salad

Main Dish

Cabbage Roll   Wagyu Steak
in Soup Stock   with Red Wine Sauce

Dessert

Chocolate Torte   Cherry Pie

All items on special for our fifth anniversary. A ten-dollar discount from the listed prices.

A. $30
B. $35
C. $40
D. $45

(Answer:)

選択肢だけ提示された問題：ダイアローグ編

＊下線部が解答のヒントになる部分です。　　　　部分の表現に気を付けましょう。本文と正解の選択肢がパラフレーズされています。

Questions 1–3

解答　1. D　2. D　3. A

スクリプト

Woman: What've you been up to lately, Marco? You've been at your desk all morning long, but it looks like you've done nothing but sipping your cuppa joe. ^{1.} Maybe, you've been hanging around with Daniel in R&D, right?

Man: No, no, Sara. I just can't get motivated. You know Lewis in Marketing? ^{2.} I happened to find out he gets double what I get. I'm proud of my work 'n' all I've done since I came here. But....

Woman: I know what you mean. ^{2.} It's too bad you feel you aren't getting what you deserve. But I heard our MP3 SUPER was based on detailed market research Lewis and his team did for three years.

Man: Yeah, I shouldn't begrudge him his reward. ^{3.} I'd better go ahead with my scheduled presentation to Moon Mart.

Questions

1. What does the woman infer about the man?

   A. He is shipping a client's order.

   B. He is wiping his desk all morning long.

   C. He has to talk to Daniel in R & D.

D. He has gone out with his coworker.

2. What does the man mean when he says, "I'm proud of my work 'n' all I've done since I came here. But..."?
   A. He doesn't feel satisfied with his performance.
   B. He regrets that he hung around with his colleague.
   C. He wants the woman to earn double.
   D He feels he should be paid as much as his colleague.

3. What is the man planning to do?
   A. Have a talk at Moon Mart
   B. Present his idea to the woman
   C. Go ahead with his marketing research
   D. Talk about MP3 SUPER

訳

Woman: 最近どうしたの、Marco？午前中ずっとデスクに座っているけどコーヒーを飲んでいるだけだし。[1.]研究開発のDanielとほっつき歩いていたんでしょ。

Man: 違うよ、Sara。やる気がでないだけさ。マーケティングのLewisを知っているだろ？[2.]やつが僕の2倍もらっていることを知っちゃったんだ。ぼくは自分の仕事やここでやってきたことにもプライドがあるし…

Woman: 言いたいことはわかるわ。[2.]思っているほど自分が評価されていないと感じてしまうのは残念だわ。でも、聞いたんだけど、わが社のMP3 SUPERはLewisと彼のチームの3年以上の詳細なマーケットリサーチのおかげだそうよ。

Man: そうだね。彼の報酬をねたんだらだめだね。[3.]スケジュールが決まっているMoon Martへのプレゼンをがんばるべきだよね。

Questions

1. 女性は男性に関して何を推測していますか？

   A. 彼はクライアントの荷物を出荷している。

   B. 彼は午前中ずっと自分のデスクを拭いている。

   C. 彼は研究開発部の Daniel と話さないといけない。

   D. 彼は同僚と出かけた。

2. "I'm proud of my work 'n' all I've done since I came here. But..."
   と男性が言っているのはどういう意味ですか？

   A. 自分のパフォーマンスに満足していない。

   B. 同僚とほっつき歩いたことを後悔している。

   C. 彼は女性に 2 倍稼いでほしい。

   D. 彼は同僚と同じくらい貰えるべきだと思っている。

3. 男性は何を予定していますか？

   A. Moon Mart で話をする。

   B. 女性に自分のアイデアをプレゼンする。

   C. 彼のマーケティングリサーチを続ける。

   D. MP3 SUPER の話をする。

ボキャブラリー hang around ぶらつく、うろつく　'n' and の省略形

参照 p. 19、p. 26、p. 29、p. 30、p. 40、p. 63、p. 90

Questions 4–6

解答　4. B　5. D　6. C

スクリプト

　　Man: Ms. Anderson, do you have a minute?

Woman: Sure, Miles. About the Thompson account?

　　Man: No, Ms. Anderson. ^{4.} <u>I need to take tomorrow afternoon off to see my dentist</u>. Usually, I see her on Thursday mornings because I have Thursday off. But ^{5.} I'm going to visit my sister next Thursday to join her son, Calvin's birthday party. Could I get a paid sick day for tomorrow's appointment?

Woman: I'm sorry, Miles. ^{6.} You cannot get sick leave until you've been here for a year. Since you only joined us this June, you are not eligible.

Questions

4. What is the man's problem?
   A. He has trouble with the Thompson account.
   B. He has a private matter to attend to during his work hours.
   C. He missed one of his afternoon assignments.
   D. He must introduce Ms. Anderson to the Thompsons.

5. What can be inferred about the man's sister?
   A. She lives with the man.
   B. She is single.
   C. She sees the man every Thursday.
   D. She has one or more children.

6. What does the woman say about sick leave?
   A. The man can get sick leave for one year.
   B. Sick leave can be taken only in June.
   C. Payment is not made for the first year.
   D. June is the first month the employees can get sick leave.

訳

Man: Ms. Anderson、今お時間ありますか？

Woman: ええ、Miles。Thompson の件？

Man: いいえ、Ms. Anderson。^{4.}明日の午後に休みを取って歯医者に

行きたいんです。普段は木曜日が休みなので、木曜に診てもら
うんですが、^{5.}次の木曜は姉のところへ行くんです。姉の息子の
Calvin の誕生日なんです。明日の歯医者の予約に有給病欠休暇
を使えますか?

Woman: ごめんね、Miles。^{6.}一年在職しないと病欠休暇はもらえないの。
あなたは6月に入ったばかりだから資格がないのよ。

Questions

4. 男性の問題は何ですか?

    A. Thompson の件でトラブルを抱えている。

    B. 就業時間中にやらないといけないプライベートなことがある。

    C. 午後の仕事をひとつやりそこねた。

    D. Ms. Anderson を Thompson さん一家に紹介しないといけない。

5. 男性の姉に関して何が推測できますか?

    A. 彼と一緒に住んでいる。

    B. 独身だ。

    C. 彼と毎週木曜日に会っている。

    D. 一人以上の子供がいる。

6. 病欠休暇に関して女性はなんと言っていますか?

    A. 彼は1年間病欠休暇を取れる。

    B. 病欠休暇は6月だけ取れる。

    C. 1年目は報酬が発生しない。

    D. 6月は従業員たちが病欠休暇をもらえる最初の月だ。

ボキャブラリー paid sick day(sick leave)有給の病欠休み　eligible 資格がある

Questions 7-9

解答　7. C　8. B　9. B

スクリプト

Woman: Excuse me. I bought this blouse here the other day. I first tried it on yesterday, but ^{7.} it didn't look so good with any of my pants or jackets. Could I exchange it? Here's the receipt.

Man: I see. Let me check, ma'am. Hmm..., I'm sorry, but I'm afraid you can't. ^{8.} You purchased this pink blouse on July 5th, which is exactly two months ago. Our return policy stipulates you can exchange any item you have bought with another item within 30 days of your purchase.

Woman: But I tried this on for the first time yesterday. I hadn't even unwrapped it until yesterday. Don't I have a right to a replacement?

Man: Sorry, ma'am. There is nothing wrong with this shirt. Since you are a regular customer, however, ^{9.} we'd like to offer you a 10% discount voucher you can use for your next purchase.

165

Questions

7. What is the woman's problem?
   A. The blouse is too small for her.
   B. She lost the receipt for the pants and the jacket.
   C. She feels none of her clothes go well with the blouse she bought.
   D. The shop doesn't have any pants or jackets to her taste.

8. What is the reason the woman can't exchange the item?
   A. She isn't sure when she bought it.
   B. She got the item too long ago.

C. She has exchanged the item before.

D. The blouse was a good bargain on July 5th.

9. What is one thing the man offers the woman?

A. Some wrapping

B. A coupon

C. A replacement

D. A defective item

訳

Woman: すみません。先日このブラウスをここで買ったんだけど、昨日初めて着てみたら、^{7.}持っているどのパンツやジャケットとも合わないの。交換できない？これがレシート。

Man: わかりました。チェックさせてください。う〜ん、すみませんが交換できません。^{8.}このピンクのブラウスを7月5日にお買い上げいただいていますが、ちょうど2か月前になります。我々の返品規約ではお買い上げ後30日以内なら他の製品と交換できるとあります。

Woman: でも、昨日初めて着たのよ。昨日までは包装も開けなかったわ。交換の資格があるんじゃないの？

Man: すみません、奥様。このシャツにはどこも悪いところはございません。しかし、奥様は私共のお得意様ですので、^{9.}次回のご購入にお使いいただける10%割引券をお渡しいたします。

Questions

7. 女性の問題は何ですか？

A. ブラウスが小さすぎる。

B. パンツとジャケットのレシートを失くした。

C. 彼女が買ったブラウスが自分のどの服とも合わないと感じている。

D. この店には彼女好みのパンツやジャケットがない。

8. 女性が品物を交換できない理由は何ですか？

　A. それをいつ買ったか確かでない。

　B. それをあまりにも以前に購入している。

　C. 前にそれを交換したことがある。

　D. そのブラウスは7月5日にお買い得品だった。

9. 男性が女性にオファーしたものは何ですか？

　A. 包装

　B. クーポン

　C. 交換品

　D. 欠陥品

ボキャブラリー stipulate（規則などで）規定する　voucher チケット、クーポン

参照 p. 19、p. 24、p. 39

167

Questions 10–12

解答　10. C　11. A　12. B

スクリプト

Man 1: We've recently had quite a few complaints about our telephone support. ^{10.}The average time it takes a caller to reach our staff is over thirty minutes. What do you think, Susan?

Woman: I know, Jake. On our web site, there're tons of similar complaints about waiting times. ^{10.}We need more representatives or longer service hours, like a night shift.

Man 1: What do you think, Greg?

Man 2: Night shift isn't a good idea. You know, it's called "the graveyard shift" for a reason – it kills you! And hiring more staff is too costly. Outsourcing our support line abroad is the only path we can take. ^{11.}We can double the number of customer service representatives because the labor cost per head is surprisingly low. Some staffing agencies can fill positions abroad for outsourced American jobs. I've read their local staff have quite a high level of expertise. There're a bunch of American IT businesses using overseas call centers.

Man 1: Outsourcing is one choice, but I wonder if those foreign call center workers have enough communication skills to deal with American users. [12.] We should look into it a little further.

Questions

10. What is the problem?
    A. Susan has complaints about their telephone support.
    B. The technical representatives repeat the same complaints.
    C. Their support line is short-staffed.
    D. They can't reach their customers on their website.

11. Why does Greg think they should outsource their support line?
    A. Because it's cost-effective.
    B. Because it will double the customers.
    C. Because he can gain some degree of expertise.
    D. Because it is called "the graveyard shift."

12. What does Jake say about outsourcing their support line?
    A. Foreign staff may not like American users.
    B. They will research it.
    C. He doubts the expertise of the support center staff.
    D. Foreign staff have enough communication skills.

Man 1: 最近テレホンサポートにたくさんの苦情が来ている。^{10.}電話を
かけている人がスタッフにつながるまでの平均時間が30分を超
えているようだ。Susan、どう思う？

Woman: 知っているわ、Jake。会社のウェブサイトにも待ち時間の苦情
がたくさん来ているわ。^{10.}もっとスタッフを増やすか、夜勤の
ような長時間サービスが必要よ。

Man 1: Greg はどう思う？

Man 2: 夜勤はいい考えじゃない。「墓場シフト」って呼ばれているって
知っているかい。「死んじゃうよ」って意味だ。スタッフをもっ
と雇うのはコストがかかりすぎるし。サポートラインを海外へ
外注に出すことが唯一の方法だ。^{11.}ひとり当りの人件費が驚くほ
ど安いからカスタマーサービスの人員を倍に増やせる。米国企業
の外注欠員を海外で補充している人材派遣会社もあるよ。人材派
遣会社の海外スタッフの専門知識はかなりレベルが高いって読ん
だことがある。海外のコールセンターを使っているアメリカのIT
企業はたくさんあるし。

Man 1: 外注も選択肢のひとつだが、海外のコールセンターの人員がアメ
リカ人ユーザーに対処するに十分なコミュニケーション力がある
かは疑問だ。^{12.}もう少し調べてみよう。

Questions

10. 問題は何ですか？

    A. Susan は自分たちのテレホンサポートに不平がある。

    B. 技術スタッフが同じ不平を繰り返す。

    C. サポートラインのスタッフが足りない。

    D. 自分たちのウェブサイトで顧客と連絡が取れない。

11. なぜ Greg はサポートラインを外注に出すべきだと思っていますか？

    A. 安上がりだから。

B. 顧客を2倍にできるから。

C. ある程度の専門知識を得られるから。

D. それが「墓場シフト」と呼ばれているから。

12. サポートラインの外注に対して Jake は何と言っていますか？

A. 外国のスタッフはアメリカ人ユーザーが好きでないかもしれない。

B. それについて調査する。

C. 彼はサポートセンタースタッフの専門知識を疑っている。

D. 外国人スタッフは十分なコミュニケーション能力を持っている。

ボキャブラリー reach（電話が）つながる outsourcing 外注、（仕事などの）外部委託 fill positions 欠員を補充する

参照 p. 18、p. 39、p. 90

Questions 13–15

解答 **13. C 14. A 15. D**

スクリプト

Woman: ¹³·Don't you think it's about time we upgraded our OS?

　　Man: Well, obviously, a newer version would be faster, but the one we're using is serving us well enough, isn't it?

Woman: Sure, we can get by on it, but if we don't get an upgrade, ¹³·¹⁴·we'll lose an edge over the competition.

　　Man: ¹⁵·Do you know how much an upgrade will cost?

Woman: No, but I'll find out.

　　Man: Great! ¹³·¹⁵·If it looks like it'll fit into next year's budget, I'll take it upstairs.

Questions

13. Where is this conversation probably taking place?

A. At a family home

B. At a church

C. At an office

D. At a warehouse

14. What is the woman's concern?

A. Losing an advantage over their rivals

B. Becoming less edgy

C. Taking the edge off

D. Their competitive nature

15. What is the man's concern?

A. The competition

B. The upstairs neighbor

C. The effectiveness of the latest OS

D. The expenses

訳

Woman: ^{13.}そろそろ OS をアップグレードする時期だと思わない？

Man: そうだね。新しいバージョンの方が速いだろうけど、今使っているものでも十分役立っているよ。

Woman: もちろんこれでもやっていけるけど、^{13. 14.}アップグレードしないとライバルより優位に立てないわ。

Man: アップグレードのコストがどれくらいかわかる？

Woman: いいえ。でも探すわ。

Man: よし。^{13. 15.}もし来年の予算に合うなら、上に掛け合ってみるよ。

Questions

13. この会話はどこでおこなわれている可能性が高いでしょうか？

A. 家庭で

B. 教会で

C. オフィスで

D. 倉庫で

14. 女性は何を心配していますか？

A. ライバル達に対して優位性が失われること。

B. イライラが少なくなること。

C. 刃先が鈍くなること。

D. 彼らの競争好きな性格

15. 男性の心配は何ですか？

A. ライバル

B. 上の階の隣人

C. 最新 OS の有効性

D. 費用

172

ボキャブラリー the competition（集合的に）競争相手、ライバル　edge 刃先、（刃のように鋭い）能力や優位性　edgy（刃先が体に触れているように）イライラした　upstairs 上層部、上司達

参照 p. 19、p. 40、p. 65、p. 71

Questions 16–18

解答　16. A　17. C　18. A

スクリプト

Man 1: [16.] Welcome to First City, Toronto. How can we help you?

Woman: [16.] I'd like to exchange some currency.

Man 1: Currency exchange is over there.

Man 2: How much would you like to exchange?

Woman: 100,000 yen.

Man 2: Here you are: 1210 dollars.

Woman: Really? I thought the exchange rate was about 102 yen to the dollar.

Man 2: [17, 18] The rate is about 102 yen to the American dollar now. However, it's 82 yen to the Canadian dollar. And there's the handling charge.

Woman: I see.

Man 2: Well, I hope you enjoy your stay here.

Woman: Thanks!

Questions

16. Where is this conversation most likely taking place?

   A. A financial institution in Canada

   B. A bank in the U.S.

   C. An exchange counter in Japan

   D. A trading company

17. What most likely is the reason the woman says, "Really? I thought the exchange rate was about 102 yen to the dollar"?

   A. Canada and the U.S. are similar countries.

   B. The rates of two currencies are similar.

   C. The names of two currencies are similar.

   D. They're communicating online.

18. What is true about the American dollar?

   A. It is more valuable than the Canadian currency.

   B. It is about the same value as the Canadian currency.

   C. It is less valuable than the Canadian currency.

   D. Its value fluctuates.

訳

Man 1: [16] First city, Toronto へようこそ。ご用件をお伺いします。

Woman: ^{16.}通貨を交換したいんです。

Man 1: 通貨交換はそちらです。

Man 2: いくら交換いたしましょうか？

Woman: 100,000円

Man 2: どうぞ。1210ドルです。

Woman: え？レートは1ドル102円と思ったのですが。

Man 2: ^{17. 18.}対アメリカドルは102円ですが、対カナダドルは82円です。それと手数料がかかります。

Woman: わかりました。

Man 2: こちらでの滞在をお楽しみください。

Woman: ありがとう。

Questions

16. この会話はどこでおこなわれている可能性が一番高いですか？
    A. カナダの金融機関
    B. アメリカの銀行
    C. 日本の通貨交換所
    D. 貿易会社

174

17. 女性が、"Really? I thought the exchange rate was about 102 yen to the dollar" と言っている最もそれらしい理由は何ですか？
    A. カナダとアメリカは似ている国だ。
    B. ふたつの通貨レートが似ている。
    C. ふたつの通貨の名前が似ている。
    D. 彼らはオンラインで話している。

18. アメリカドルについて真実はどれですか？
    A. カナダの通貨より価値が高い。
    B. カナダの通貨と価値が同じだ。
    C. カナダの通貨より価値が低い。

D. 価値が変動する。

ボキャブラリー First City 首都など、その国で一番重要な都市　currency exchange
通貨交換　financial institute 金融機関

参照　p. 55、p. 93

Questions 19-21
解答　19. A　20. B　21. C

スクリプト

　　Man: Hello, Asiatic Travel. ^{19.}Thank you for holding. How can I help you?

Woman: Well, I'd like to book a trip to Europe.

　　Man: When are you thinking of going?

Woman: Soon after Easter. ^{20.}Whenever I can get a good deal on flights and hotels.

　　Man: Okay...Which countries do you want to visit?

Woman: The UK and France.

　　Man: And how long would you like to stay for?

Woman: About ten days.

　　Man: Well, I can get you a package tour. Five days in London, cross the Channel, and another five days in Paris. 450,000 yen. How does that sound?

Woman: Pretty good....Do I have to join a guided tour every day?

　　Man: No, you don't.

Woman: Good. All right. ^{21.}Could you email me the dates, price and what's covered?

　　Man: Certainly.

Questions

19. Where is this conversation most likely taking place?

175

A. On the phone

B. At the travel agency

C. By instant message

D. By email

20. What can we infer about the woman?

    A. She has people who can show her around London and Paris.

    B. She is a bargain hunter.

    C. She speaks French.

    D. She loves cable TV channels.

21. What does the woman request of the man?

    A. To join a guided tour

    B. To take a tour of the Channel

    C. To contact her later

    D. To e-mail her during Easter

訳

Man: はい、Asiatic Travel です。 19. お電話お待ちいただきありがとう
ございます。どのようなご用件でしょうか?

Woman: ヨーロッパ旅行の予約をしたいのですが。

Man: いつ頃をお考えですか?

Woman: 復活祭の直後くらいです。 20. フライトとホテルがお得な時なら
いつでもいいです。

Man: わかりました。どの国をご希望ですか?

Woman: イギリスとフランスです。

Man: 何日のご予定ですか?

Woman: 10日くらいです。

Man: パッケージツアーをお取りできます。ロンドンで5日間、英仏海
峡を越えて、パリで5日間。450,000円です。いかがでしょうか?

Woman: いいですね…　毎日ガイドツアーに参加しないといけないですか？

Man: いいえ。その必要はありません。

Woman: それは良かったです。^{21.} <u>日時、料金と何が含まれているかメールいただけますか？</u>

Man: 承知しました。

Questions

19. この会話はどこでおこなわれている可能性が一番高いですか？
    - A. 電話
    - B. 旅行代理店
    - C. インスタントメッセージ
    - D. メール

20. 女性に関して何が推測できますか？
    - A. 彼女にはロンドンとパリを案内してくれる人がいる。
    - B. 彼女は格安を狙う人だ。
    - C. 彼女はフランス語を話す。
    - D. 彼女はケーブルテレビ番組が好きだ。

21. 女性は男性に何をリクエストしていますか？
    - A. ガイドツアーに参加すること。
    - B. 海峡ツアーをすること。
    - C. 後で彼女に連絡すること。
    - D. 復活祭の間に彼女にメールすること。

ボキャブラリー　bargain hunter　お買い得品を積極的に探す人

参照　p. 18、p. 55、p. 65、p. 71

Questions 22-24

解答　22. B　23. C　24.C

スクリプト

Woman: ^{22.} I hope you've all had a chance to look at the bar chart our department has handed out. It concerns, primarily, of course, the sales of spring/summer wear. Any questions or comments?

Man 1: Do sales usually peak in June?

Woman: ^{23.} Probably.

Man 1: Why's that? The beginning of summer sales?

Woman: ^{23.} That might be a big reason.

Man 2: The discounts continue in July, don't they?

Woman: Yes, they do.

Man 2: Are the discounts in July bigger than those in June?

Woman: ^{23.} You know, I don't know − I'll have to check.

Man 1: Not for the clothes in my section.

Man 2: ^{24.} And why do sales drop off so dramatically in August?

Woman: Well, I guess it's one of those in-between months. People have their summer clothes, but it's too early to think about the fall yet.

Man 1: How could we get feedback on that?

Woman: ^{24.} Well, could you research this? Find out the best way to get into our customers' heads.

Man 1: ^{24.} Sure.

Woman: Okay. Let's meet again in a week and decide what adjustments we need to make, if any.

Questions

22. Who is most likely the woman?

   A. A salesclerk

B. The sales manager

C. The company president

D. A manufacturer

23. What can we infer about the woman?

A. She is very prepared.

B. She needs to listen to her subordinates' suggestions.

C. She is not as prepared as she could be.

D. She is more prepared than she needs to be.

24. What will probably be discussed at the next meeting?

A. Why sales fall so dramatically in August and how to provide better service.

B. Why sales fall so dramatically in July and how to provide better service.

C. Why sales fall so dramatically in August and how to understand the customers better.

D. When to put fall clothes on display.

訳

Woman: ²² 我が部から配布された棒グラフは見てくれたと思います。もちろん主に春夏服の売り上げに関するものです。何か質問かコメントがありますか？

Man 1: 売り上げはいつも6月がピークですか？

Woman: ²³ おそらく。

Man 1: なぜですか？サマーセールが始まるからですか？

Woman: ²³ それも大きな理由かもしれません。

Man 2: ディスカウントは7月も続きますよね。

Woman: そうですね。

Man 2: 7月のディスカウント額は6月より大きいのですか？

Woman: ²³·わかりません。チェックしてみます。

Man 1: うちの部の服はそうじゃないですね。

Man 2: ²⁴·それと、なぜ売り上げが8月に劇的に落ちるのでしょう?

Woman: そうですね。中間月だからじゃないでしょうか。夏服は持っているし、秋物にはまだ早いし。

Man 1: どのようにフィードバックをもらえますか?

Woman: ²⁴·そうですね。それを調べてもらえますか?顧客が何を欲しているかを知るベストな方法を見つけてください。

Man 1: ²⁴·わかりました。

Woman: では1週間後にまた集まって、何を調整すべきか決めましょう。

Questions

22. 女性は誰でしょうか?

    A. 販売員

    B. 営業部長

    C. 社長

    D. 製造業者

23. 女性について何が推測できますか?

    A. 彼女は準備がよくできている。

    B. 彼女は部下の提案をよく聞く必要がある。

    C. 彼女は準備がよくできていない。

    D. 彼女は必要以上に準備ができている。

24. 次のミーティングで何が議論されるでしょうか?

    A. 8月に売り上げが劇的に落ちる理由とよりよいサービスを提供する方法。

    B. 7月に売り上げが劇的に落ちる理由とよりよいサービスを提供する方法。

    C. 8月に売り上げが劇的に落ちる理由と顧客をよりよく理解する方法。

D. いつ秋物をディスプレーするか。

ボキャブラリー in-between 中間の
参照 p. 38、p. 41、p. 65

Questions 25−27
解答 25. B 26. D 27. A
スクリプト

Woman: First, let's make a list.

　　Man: Wait. Let me get a pen. Okay. Go.

Woman: ^{25.} Well, how about two large steaks?

　　Man: That should do it. Do we need sauce?

Woman: No, we're good. A small bag of potatoes.

　　Man: Are we going to make mashed potatoes?

Woman: Yeah, let's! Do we have enough butter?

　　Man: We do, but we need a carton of milk.

Woman: And salad materials: a couple of tomatoes, a head of lettuce, a can of tuna.

　　Man: Got it. We have salad dressing. Should we get mayonnaise in case anyone wants some?

Woman: Good idea. What about drinks?

　　Man: ^{26. 27.} Well, I told them it's BYOB, so we don't have to go to the liquor store. We're providing coffee, of course.

Woman: And dessert?

　　Man: ^{27.} Fred and Mary promised to bring something.

Questions

25. What can we infer about the guests?

　　A. They do not eat mayonnaise.

　　B. They are not vegetarians.

C. They are allergic to dairy products.

D. They are on a diet.

26. What can be inferred about the speakers?

A. They will be serving alcohol.

B. They will be serving tea.

C. They won't be serving their guests anything to drink.

D. They won't be serving alcohol to their guests.

27. What, probably, is the situation?

A. A couple is entertaining friends.

B. Business associates are entertaining clients.

C. Classmates are planning a study session.

D. Parents are entertaining their children.

182

訳

Woman: 先にリストを作りましょう。

Man: 待って。ペンを持ってくる。さあ、いいよ。

Woman: ^{25.} そうね。大きなステーキ2枚はどう？

Man: いいね。ソースは要る？

Woman: いいえ。十分あるわ。ジャガイモの小袋をひとつ。

Man: マッシュポテトを作るかい？

Woman: ええ、そうしましょう！バターは十分あった？

Man: あるよ。ミルクは買わないと。

Woman: サラダの材料も必要ね。トマト、レタスとツナ1缶ね。

Man: わかった。ドレッシングはあるし。誰かが欲しがった時のために
マヨネーズを買っとく？

Woman: それはいいわね。飲み物はどうする？

Man: ^{26. 27.} BYOB って言ってあるから酒屋さんに行かなくてもいいよ。
もちろんコーヒーはこっちで出すよ。

Woman: デザートは？

Man: Fred と Mary が持ってくるって約束してくれたよ。

Questions

25. ゲストについて何が推測できますか？
    A. 彼らはマヨネーズを食べない。
    B. 彼らはベジタリアン（菜食主義）ではない。
    C. 彼らは乳製品にアレルギーがある。
    D. 彼らはダイエット中だ。

26. 話し手たちについて何が推測できますか？
    A. 彼らはアルコールを提供する。
    B. 彼らはお茶を提供する。
    C. 彼らはゲストに飲み物を何も提供しない。
    D. 彼らはゲストにアルコールを提供しない。

27. この状況はおそらく次のどれですか？
    A. カップルが友達をもてなそうとしている。
    B. 仕事仲間がクライアントをもてなそうとしている。
    C. クラスメートが勉強会を催そうとしている。
    D. 両親が子供をもてなそうとしている。

ボキャブラリー good 十分ある

参照 p. 18

Questions 28−30
解答　28. C　29. A　30.B

スクリプト

Woman: Excuse me, do you have a table available for five? I'm
afraid we didn't make a reservation.

Man: Sorry ma'am. ^{28.} A party of 20 is taking up half of this restaurant now. We don't have any tables available at the moment. We can arrange a table for five in an hour, though.

Woman: Well, I don't think we can find another restaurant to our taste near here. Could you show me the menu?

Man: Of course, ma'am. Here you are. Today, we have two dinner specials. ^{29., 30.} We offer them for special prices today and tomorrow only, because tomorrow is our fifth anniversary.

Woman: Wow. They're awesome. Cabbage Roll or Wagyu steak. I can't choose one.... ^{30.} Oh, I don't eat burdock, so I'll choose the other one. Could we order five of this set? We'll come back in an hour.

Questions

28. Why is the restaurant full now?
    A. Because twenty parties are held at the same time.
    B. Because they are celebrating their 20th anniversary.
    C. Because a large group is occupying many tables.
    D. Because regular staff are not available today.

29. What does the man say about the special offers?
    A. They are for a limited time.
    B. They are for his fifth wedding anniversary.
    C. The restaurant serves different dinners every day.
    D. They are not on the menu.

30. Look at the menu. How much will each member of the woman's party pay?

```
┌─────────────────────────────────────────────────┐
│              Today's  Menu                        │
│   Set Menu A $40              Set Menu B $45       │
│                  Appetizer                         │
│   Marinated Tomato        Eggplant Pickles         │
│                    Soup                            │
│   Pescador Onion Soup     Spanish Garlic Soup      │
│                    Salad                           │
│   Burdock Salad           Caesar Salad             │
│                  Main Dish                         │
│   Cabbage Roll            Wagyu Steak              │
│   in Soup Stock           with Red Wine Sauce      │
│                   Dessert                          │
│   Chocolate Torte         Cherry Pie               │
│                                                    │
│   All items on special for our fifth anniversary. A ten- │
│   dollar discount from the listed prices.          │
└─────────────────────────────────────────────────┘
```

A. $30

B. $35

C. $40

D. $45

訳

Woman: すみません。5人ですが、席がありますか?予約はしていないんですが。

Man: すみません。今20名様のグループがレストランの半分を使っておられます。今ご用意できる席はございません。1時間でご用意はできますが。

Woman: この近くで口に合うレストランを見つけられなさそうだし。メ

ニューを見せてもらえますか？

Man: かしこまりました。どうぞ。本日は2種類のディナーをご用意しております。明日が5周年になりますので、今日と明日だけスペシャルプライスで提供させていただいております。

Woman: わー、おいしそう。ロールキャベツと和牛ステーキね。選べないわ… あ、私ごぼうが食べられないから、もう片方にします。このセットを5つお願いします。1時間で帰ってきます。

Questions

28. なぜレストランは今満席ですか？

A. パーティーが20組同時におこなわれているから。

B. レストランが20周年記念を祝っているから。

C. 大グループが多くの席を独占しているから。

D. 今日はレギュラーのスタッフがいないから。

29. スペシャルオファーについて男性は何を言っていますか？

A. 期間が限られている。

B. 彼の結婚5周年を記念している。

C. レストランは毎日違ったディナーを提供している。

D. それらはメニューに載っていない。

30. メニューを見てください。この女性のメンバー各々はいくら支払いますか？

本日のメニュー	
セットメニュー A $40	セットメニュー B $45
前菜	
トマトマリネ	茄子のピクルス
スープ	
漁師風オニオンスープ	スペイン風ガーリックスープ

サラダ

ごぼうサラダ　　　　　　　シーザーサラダ

メインディッシュ

出汁入りロールキャベツ　　和牛ステーキ赤ワインソース

デザート

チョコレートトルテ　　　　チェリーパイ

5周年スペシャルです。メニューの値段から10ドル割引になります。

A. $30

B. $35

C. $40

D. $45

参照 p. 60、P. 66

2. 問題と選択肢が提示された問題：モノローグ編

Questions 1 – 3 （Public Announcement） 🔊 **Track 62**

1. Where is the announcement most likely being made?

   A. At a school

   B. At an amusement park

   C. At a department store

   D. At a corner store

   （Answer:　）

2. What can be inferred about the girl?

   A. She likes going shopping with her mother.

   B. She hasn't given out any of her personal information yet.

   C. She lost her purse.

   D. She hasn't visited the place before.

   （Answer:　）

3. What will most likely happen next?

   A. Security guards will take her upstairs.

   B. All the elevators will stop at the basement.

   C. The little girl will go to the basement by herself.

   D. The child will see a member of her family.

   （Answer:　）

Questions 4 – 6 （Telephone Message） 🔊 **Track 63**

4. What is the message about?

    A. Saturday School

    B. A casual gathering

    C. An invitation to the lecture about BYOB

    D. A family outing

（Answer: ）

5. What can be inferred about Jean and Tom?

    A. They go to the same school.

    B. They recently met around the intersection.

    C. They once lived together on 50th Avenue.

    D. They have got lost at Cambie before.

（Answer: ）

6. What can be inferred about the location mentioned?

    A. It is east on Cambie.

    B. It is half-way down South Avenue.

    C. Jean has been to the place before.

    D. Tom lives half-way down the place.

（Answer: ）

Questions 7 – 9 （Excerpt from a meeting） 🔊 **Track 64**

7. What does the speaker want all the participants in the meeting to do?

    A. Think about their long-term goals

    B. Make plans for the coming calendar year

    C. Make plans for the next business year

    D. Think about their studies

（Answer: ）

8. This meeting is probably being held in:

   A. March

   B. April

   C. June

   D. December

   （Answer:　）

9. Who most likely is speaking?

   A. A clerk

   B. A teacher

   C. A manager

   D. A consultant

   （Answer:　）

Questions 10 – 12　（Telephone Message）　◁» **Track 65**

10. Why does the speaker leave this message?

   A. Because Erika likes eggs and chocolate cake.

   B. Because eggs are essential to make chocolate cake.

   C. Because George forgot to buy eggs yesterday.

   D. Because she wants to serve eggs for the celebrations.

   （Answer:　）

11. What can we infer from the message?

   A. Tomorrow is Erika's christening.

   B. Tomorrow is Erika's birthday.

   C. Tomorrow is Erika's graduation.

   D. Tomorrow is Erika's entrance ceremony.

   （Answer:　）

12. What ingredient can we infer the woman has enough of at home?

A. Eggs

B. Whipped cream

C. Sprinkles

D. Butter

(Answer:)

Questions 13 – 15 （Public Announcement） 🔊 **Track 66**

13. What can we infer from this announcement?

A. The economic situation is serious.

B. A natural disaster is occurring.

C. The listeners want to relocate to another city.

D. Emergency crews are driving too fast.

(Answer:)

14. Where most likely is this announcement made?

A. At a city center

B. Near a body of water

C. Near the bureau of waterworks

D. Near a mountain peak

(Answer:)

15. How can we infer that most people should reach higher ground?

A. On foot

B. By motorcycle

C. By bicycle

D. By ambulance

(Answer:)

Questions 16 – 18 (Telephone Message) 🔊 **Track 67**

16. What did the speaker most likely do last week?

    A. He got a managerial position.

    B. He met one or more candidates.

    C. He was hired by Hi End Electronics.

    D. He worked with the technical support team.

                      （Answer:　）

17. Why did the speaker leave this message?

    A. He wanted to know about the details of an applicant.

    B. He wanted to ask about some IT corporations.

    C. He wanted to contact an applicant for a position.

    D. He used to work for the IT corporation the interviewee had worked for.

                      （Answer:　）

18. What is most likely to happen after March 3rd?

    A. Hi End Electronics would offer a candidate a position in Asia.

    B. Hi End Electronics might not hire the applicant they called.

    C. Hi End Electronics would expand business in Asia.

    D. Hi End Electronics might reduce the number of their technical support members.

                      （Answer:　）

Questions 19 – 21 (News Report) 🔊 **Track 68**

19. What happened on the West Coast yesterday?

    A. Bad weather negatively influenced the local people.

    B. A raging storm struck the area on a record-breaking hot day.

    C. A storm struck many damaged or destroyed houses left behind by their previous residents.

    D. The residents of the area watched a movie titled "A Day of Terror."

                           (Answer:)

20. What is true about the storm?

    A. It killed at least 40 people.

    B. It caused serious damage to the buildings near the sea.

    C. Strong winds blew but the rain was not heavy.

    D. It hardly caused destruction of life and property.

                           (Answer:)

21. What did the government spokesman announce?

    A. The government will give away some money to the victims.

    B. The government will benefit from the storm.

    C. The government will establish a bank to support the sufferers.

    D. The government will avoid catastrophic damage to be caused by a major earthquake.

                           (Answer:)

Questions 22 – 24 （Excerpt from a meeting） 🔊 **Track 69**

22. Who are the listeners?

    A. Business owners

    B. Consultants

    C. Managing staff

    D. Authors

                                 （Answer: ）

23. What is the theme of the talk?

    A. How to make consulting successful

    B. How to have an effective meeting

    C. How to deal with part-time employees

    D. How to avoid annoyances during lunch

                                 （Answer: ）

24. What does the speaker say about lunch?

    A. It is after the panel discussion.

    B. Not everyone can eat at the facility in the venue.

    C. Lunch sold in delis needs a few minutes to prepare.

    D. The participants will eat lunch with Alan Chung.

                                 （Answer: ）

Questions 25 – 27 （Broadcast） 🔊 **Track 70**

25. Who is the speaker?

    A. A TV news anchor

    B. A radio broadcaster

    C. A magazine reporter

    D. A real estate agent

                                 （Answer: ）

26. Why does the speaker say, "Now, let's get down to business"?
    A. To begin to talk about housing in Japan
    B. To explain "cookie-cutter housing" in North America
    C. To compare "cookie-cutter housing" with Japanese housing style
    D. To warn them not to buy a house in downtown Tokyo

    （Answer:　）

27. What is most likely the topic of the coming talk?
    A. Getting a position at a Japanese bank
    B. Dealing with financial institutions
    C. Taking out a loan from real estate agents
    D. Applying grease on one's elbows

    （Answer:　）

Questions 28 – 30 （Excerpt from a meeting） ◁») **Track 71**

28. What can be inferred about the seafood business from the talk?
    A. Some commercial fisheries use skyrockets to catch fish.
    B. Sales reps catch and sell fishery resources themselves to meet their customer demands.
    C. Consumers eat more seafood than before.
    D. Some fishing boats have the satellite network system.

    （Answer:　）

29. Look at the handout. Which of the following does the speaker want to promote most?

Fish Item	Cod	Sardines	Salmon	Herring
Net sales (tns.)	100	130	320	290

    A. Cod

    B. Salmon

    C. Herring

    D. Sardines

（Answer:　）

30. What does the speaker want the listeners to do?

    A. To give her their research results

    B. To get feedback from consumers

    C. To tell her their preference of seafood

    D. To conduct a consumer survey

（Answer:　）

解答

選択肢だけが提示された問題：モノローグ編

* 下線部が解答のヒントになる部分です。　　　部分の表現に気を付けましょう。本文と正解の選択肢がパラフレーズされています。

Questions 1–3 （放送）

解答　1. C　2. B　3. D

スクリプト

^{1.}Attention, shoppers. ^{3.}A little girl has lost her mother. ^{2.}She seems to be about three years old. She is wearing a purple dress, white tights and black shoes. ^{2.}Unfortunately, she is too shy to give her name. If this is your little girl, ^{1. 3.}please go to the security office by the north elevators in the basement.

Questions

1. Where is the announcement most likely being made?

    A. At a school

    B. At an amusement park

    C. At a department store

    D. At a corner store

2. What can be inferred about the girl?

    A. She likes going shopping with her mother.

    B. She hasn't given out any of her personal information yet.

    C. She lost her purse.

    D. She hasn't visited the place before.

3. What will most likely happen next?

    A. Security guards will take her upstairs.

    B. All the elevators will stop at the basement.

    C. The little girl will go to the basement by herself.

    D. The child will see a member of her family.

訳

[1.] お客様にお知らせします。[3.] 小さな女の子がお母さんとはぐれました。[2.] 3歳くらいの女の子です。紫のドレス、白タイツに黒い靴を履かれています。[2.] 恥ずかしくて名前を言いません。[1.3.] 心当たりの方は地階、北エレベーター横の警備室へお越しください。

Questions

1. この放送はどこでおこなわれている可能性が高いですか？

    A. 学校

    B. 遊園地

    C. デパート

    D. 街角の食糧雑貨店

2. 女の子に関して何が推測できますか？

    A. お母さんと買い物するのが好きだ。

    B. 彼女の個人情報を何も明かしていない。

    C. 財布を失くした。

    D. ここへ来たことがない。

3. この次に何が起こる可能性が一番高いですか？

    A. 警備員が女の子を上の階に連れていく。

    B. すべてのエレベーターが地下で止まる。

    C. 女の子が一人で地下に行く。

    D. 子供が家族の人に会う。

参照 p. 18、p. 30、p. 66

Questions 4–6 （電話メッセージ）

解答 4. B 5. A 6. C

スクリプト

Jean, it's Tom. Wanted to invite you over on Saturday. ^{4.} <u>Bring a friend if you like.</u> Eight o'clock. ^{4. 5.} <u>There'll be lots of people there from school.</u> Oh, and it's BYOB. ^{6.} <u>Remember how to get to our place?</u> Once you're at the intersection of Cambie and 50th, turn east onto 50th. It'll be half-way down the block on the south side.

Questions

4. What is the message about?
   A. Saturday School
   B. A casual gathering
   C. An invitation to the lecture about BYOB
   D. A family outing

5. What can be inferred about Jean and Tom?
   A. They go to the same school.
   B. They recently met around the intersection.
   C. They once lived together on 50th Avenue.
   D. They have got lost at Cambie before.

6. What can be inferred about the location mentioned?
   A. It is east on Cambie.
   B. It is half-way down South Avenue.
   C. Jean has been to the place before.
   D. Tom lives half-way down the place.

Jean、Tom だ。土曜日に君を招待したいんだ。^{4.}よかったら友達も連れて
きてよ。8時だ。^{4.5.}学校からもたくさん来るよ。それと、BYOB だから。
^{6.}道順は憶えている？ Cambie と50番の交差点に来たら東に折れて50番
に入るんだ。半ブロック下って南側だ。

Questions

4. 何のメッセージですか？
   A. 土曜学校
   B. カジュアルな集まり
   C. BYBO についての講義への招待
   D. 家族のお出かけ

5. Jean と Tom について何が推測できますか？
   A. 同じ学校に行っている。
   B. 最近交差点の近くで会った。
   C. 昔50番街で一緒に暮らしていた。
   D. 前に Cambie で道に迷ったことがある。

6. この場所に関して何が推測できますか？
   A. Cambie の東側にある。
   B. South Avenue を半分下った所にある。
   C. Jean はここに行ったことがある。
   D. Tom はここを半分下った所に住んでいる。

参照 p. 62

Questions 7-9 (会議の抜粋)

解答 7. C 8. A 9. C

スクリプト

7. 8. Before the next fiscal year begins, I want each of you to take some time to think about your objectives. What technical skills do you want to work on in the next year? Do you plan to undertake any professional development? If so, what? Would you like to change anything about your working style? For example, would you prefer to telecommute once a week? I'm not promising that you'll get everything you ask for, but 9. we on the management team will certainly consider any suggestion you have that you think would help you be more productive. Finally, don't forget to think about down time! I won't need exact dates next week, but it would be helpful to know roughly when you'd like to take a vacation.

Questions

7. What does the speaker want all the participants in the meeting to do?
   A. Think about their long-term goals
   B. Make plans for the coming calendar year
   C. Make plans for the next business year
   D. Think about their studies

8. This meeting is probably being held in:
   A. March
   B. April
   C. June
   D. December

9. Who most likely is speaking?

A. A clerk

B. A teacher

C. A manager

D. A consultant

訳

7. 8. 次の会計年度が始まる前に、各自の目標について考えてください。来年度にはどんな技術を身につけたいのか？何かプロフェッショナルな能力開発に着手するのか？するならば何に？ワーキング・スタイルの何かを変えたいのか？例えば、週に一度在宅勤務にするのか？ 9. 我々マネジメントチームは皆さんの要望すべてに応える約束はできませんが、皆さんがより生産的になるために助けになると思っていることを考慮に入れます。最後に、休暇のことも考えておいてください。正確な日にちは来週までに必要ないですが、大体いつ頃に休暇を取りたいか知らせてもらえると助かります。

Questions

7. 話し手はミーティングの参加者に何をしてほしいですか？

    A. 長期の目的を考えること。

    B. 来年のプランを立てること。

    C. 次の会計年度のプランを考えること。

    D. 自分たちの研究について考えること。

8. このミーティングがおこなわれているのは、

    A. 3月

    B. 4月

    C. 6月

    D. 12月

9. 誰が話している可能性が一番高いですか？

    A. 職員

B. 教師

C. 管理職

D. コンサルタント

ボキャブラリー undertake professional developments プロフェッショナルな能力開発に着手する

参照 p. 60、p. 66、p. 70、p. 76、p. 96

Questions 10–12（テレフォンメッセージ）

解答 10. B 11. B 12. D

スクリプト

[10. 12.] George, can you pick up some eggs on your way home tonight? Erika wants a chocolate cake for the celebrations tomorrow. [12.] Oh, and whipped cream. If the supermarket's out of whipped cream, get some sprinkles. [11.] Candles of course. Oh, and wrapping paper. Nothing too tacky, please! [11.] All her friends will be here.

Questions

10. Why does the speaker leave this message?

    A. Because Erika likes eggs and chocolate cake.

    B. Because eggs are essential to make chocolate cake.

    C. Because George forgot to buy eggs yesterday.

    D. Because she wants to serve eggs for the celebrations.

11. What can we infer from the message?

    A. Tomorrow is Erika's christening.

    B. Tomorrow is Erika's birthday.

    C. Tomorrow is Erika's graduation.

    D. Tomorrow is Erika's entrance ceremony.

203

12. What ingredient can we infer the woman has enough of at home?
    A. Eggs
    B. Whipped cream
    C. Sprinkles
    D. Butter

訳

^{10. 12.}George、今晩帰りに玉子を買ってきてくれない？ Erika が明日のお祝いにチョコレートケーキがほしいって言うの。^{12.}あ、それとホイップクリームもね。スーパーにホイップクリームがなければスプリンクルでもいいわ。^{11.}もちろんキャンドルも。あ、それとラッピングペーパー。ダサすぎるのはだめよ。^{11.}友達がみんな来るんだから。

Questions

10. なぜ話し手はこのメッセージを残していますか？
    A. Erika が玉子とチョコレートケーキが好きだから。
    B. チョコレートケーキを作るために玉子が要るから。
    C. George が昨日たまごを買い忘れたから。
    D. お祝いで玉子を出したいから。

11. このメッセージから何が推測できますか？
    A. 明日は Erika の洗礼式だ。
    B. 明日は Erika の誕生日だ。
    C. 明日は Erika の卒業式だ。
    D. 明日は Erika の入学式だ。

12. 女性はどの材料を家に十分持っていると推測できますか？
    A. たまご
    B. ホイップクリーム

C. スプリンクル

D. バター

ボキャブラリー sprinkle（クッキーやクリームに振りかける）粒チョコレート

参照 p. 30、p. 55、p. 76

Questions 13–15（放送）

解答 13. B 14. B 15. A

スクリプト

13.14.Attention, the levee was broken in several places in last night's storm and a flood is approaching quickly! Leave your buildings immediately and go to higher ground. 15.Do not attempt to drive, as the roads may be blocked. If you are unable to leave your building, try to get to the roof. If you cannot do that, wave or hang a white towel outside your window and emergency crews will attempt to help you relocate.

Questions

13. What can we infer from this announcement?

　　A. The economic situation is serious.

　　B. A natural disaster is occurring.

　　C. The listeners want to relocate to another city.

　　D. Emergency crews are driving too fast.

14. Where most likely is this announcement made?

　　A. At a city center

　　B. Near a body of water

　　C. Near the bureau of waterworks

　　D. Near a mountain peak

15. How can we infer that most people should reach higher ground?

    A. On foot

    B. By motorcycle

    C. By bicycle

    D. By ambulance

訳

[13. 14.] お知らせします！昨夜の豪雨で堤防が数カ所決壊しました。洪水が急激に近づいています。すぐに建物を出て高いところへ向かってください。[15.] 車は使わないでください。道路が遮断されるかもしれません。建物から出られないなら屋根に上がってください。上がれないなら白い布を窓から振るか結びつけてください。緊急救援隊が移動を手伝います。

Questions

13. 放送から何が推測できますか？

    A. 経済状況が深刻だ。

    B. 自然災害が起こっている。

    C. 聞き手は他の都市に移転しようとしている。

    D. 緊急救助隊が車のスピードを出しすぎる。

14. この放送はどこでされている可能性が一番高いですか？

    A. 都心

    B. 水域の近く

    C. 水道局の近く

    D. 山の頂上の近く

15. ほとんどの人は高い場所へどのように移動すると推測されますか？

    A. 徒歩

    B. オートバイ

    C. 自転車

D. 救急車

ボキャブラリー emergency crew 緊急救助隊員　relocate 移転する、移動する
the bureau of waterworks 水道局、ambulance 救急車

参照　p. 59

Questions 16–18（テレフォンメッセージ）
解答　16. B　17. C　18. B

スクリプト

Hello, Ms. Caroline Allison? This is Mike Smith from Hi End Electronics. ^{16.} I'm calling about the position you interviewed for last week. Thank you for being interested in the managerial position for our technical support team. We were deeply impressed with your expertise and the experience you had at several IT corporations over the past decade. As for your request to work in Asia, we can discuss it in the future. ^{17.} I sent e-mails to the address on your resume several times, but I haven't received a reply from you yet. ^{18.} We have two other candidates for the position. Could you contact us either by phone or e-mail no later than March 3rd?

Questions

16. What did the speaker most likely do last week?

　A. He got a managerial position.

　B. He met one or more candidates.

　C. He was hired by Hi End Electronics.

　D. He worked with the technical support team.

17. Why did the speaker leave this message?

　A. He wanted to know about the details of an applicant.

　B. He wanted to ask about some IT corporations.

C. He wanted to contact an applicant for a position.

D. He used to work for the IT corporation the interviewee had worked for.

18. What is most likely to happen after March 3rd?

A. Hi End Electronics would offer a candidate a position in Asia.

B. Hi End Electronics might not hire the applicant they called.

C. Hi End Electronics would expand business in Asia.

D. Hi End Electronics might reduce the number of their technical support members.

訳

Caroline Allison さんですか？ Hi End Electronics の Mike Smith です。$^{16.}$先週面接でお越しいただいた仕事の件でお電話しています。我が社のテクニカルサポートチームのマネージャー職に興味を持っていただきありがとうございます。過去10年間、いくつかの IT 企業で培われたあなたの専門知識と経験に深い感銘を受けました。アジアで働きたいという希望に関しては後ほど話し合えると思います。$^{17.}$履歴書のアドレスに何回かメールをしたのですが、まだ返信をいただいていません。$^{18.}$今回の仕事には他に2名の候補者がいます。遅くとも3月3日までに電話かメールで連絡いただけますか？

Questions

16. 話し手は、先週何をした可能性が一番高いですか？

A. 彼は管理職の仕事を得た。

B. 彼はひとり以上の候補者に会った。

C. 彼は Hi End Electronics に雇われた。

D. 彼はテクニカルサポートチームと仕事をした。

17. なぜ、話し手はこのメッセージを残しましたか？

A. 彼は候補者についての詳細を知りたかった。

B. 彼は、いくつかの IT 企業について知りたかった。

C. 彼は、仕事の候補者に連絡したかった。

D. 彼は、インタビューを受けた人が働いていた IT 企業で以前働いていた。

18. 3月3日の後、何が起こる可能性が一番高いですか？

A. Hi End Electronics が、候補者にアジアでの仕事をオファーする。

B. Hi End Electronics が、電話をかけた候補者を雇用しない。

C. Hi End Electronics が、ビジネスをアジアに拡張する。

D. Hi End Electronics が、テクニカルサポートの人員を減らす。

参照　p. 18、p. 31、p. 66、p. 76

Questions 19–21（ニュース）

解答　19. A　20. B　21.A

スクリプト

And now, for the local news. [19.] A category five hurricane struck the West Coast regions yesterday. Residents of the area experienced a day of terror. The record-breaking storm has left behind tremendous destruction, which could mean years of rebuilding. Blustery winds and downpours killed at least five people and injured 20 or more. [20.] Emergency officials say more than 40 percent of homes along the coast were destroyed or damaged. They are still trying to assess the catastrophic damage the tropical storm caused. [21.] The government spokesman announced this morning the establishment of the Disaster Fund to financially support the victims.

Questions

19. What happened on the West Coast yesterday?

A. Bad weather negatively influenced the local people.

B. A raging storm struck the area on a record-breaking hot day.

C. A storm struck many damaged or destroyed houses left behind by their previous residents.

D. The residents of the area watched a movie titled "A Day of Terror."

20. What is true about the storm?

A. It killed at least 40 people.

B. It caused serious damage to the buildings near the sea.

C. Strong winds blew but the rain was not heavy.

D. It hardly caused destruction of life and property.

21. What did the government spokesman announce?

A. The government will give away some money to the victims.

B. The government will benefit from the storm.

C. The government will establish a bank to support the sufferers.

D. The government will avoid catastrophic damage to be caused by a major earthquake.

訳

ローカルニュースの時間です。 ¹⁹·カテゴリー5のハリケーンが昨日 West Coast 地域を襲いました。住民達は恐怖の１日を経験しました。この記録破りの暴風雨はすさまじい破壊を残しました。再建に数年を要するかも知れません。暴風と豪雨で少なくとも５人が死亡し20人以上が負傷しました。²⁰·緊急事態担当官によると、海岸沿いの40% 以上の家が全壊か半壊したようです。この熱帯暴風雨がもたらした破壊的損失はまだ調査中です。²¹·今朝、政府報道官は被害に遭った人々を財政的に支援するための災害基金の設立を発表しました。

Questions

19. West Coast で昨日何が起こりましたか？

    A. 悪天候が地元住民に悪い影響をもたらした。

    B. 荒れ狂った嵐が、記録破りの暑い日にこの地域を襲った。

    C. 暴風雨が、以前住んでいた住民達が破壊して残していった家々を襲った。

    D. この地域の住民達が「恐怖の1日」というタイトルの映画を観た。

20. 暴風雨について何が真実ですか？

    A. 少なくとも40人が犠牲になった。

    B. 海に近い建物に深刻な損害をもたらした。

    C. 強い風は吹いたが、雨は激しくなかった。

    D. 人命を奪ったり家屋を破壊することはほとんどなかった。

21. 政府報道官は何を発表しましたか？

    A. 政府は犠牲者にお金を配布する。

    B. 政府は暴風雨で利益を得る。

    C. 政府は被害者を支援するために銀行を設立する。

    D. 政府は大地震で引き起こされるであろう破壊的な損害を回避するだろう。

ボキャブラリー category five ハリケーンの強さの単位。1〜5で5は最強　blustery wind 暴風　downpour 豪雨　catastrophic damage 破壊的な損害　fund 基金

参照 p. 69

Questions 22–24（ミーティングからの抜粋）

解答　22. C　23. B　24. B

スクリプト

Hello, everyone. I am Ed Nielsen from ACE Consulting. ^{23.} <u>Today, I</u>

will speak on holding a successful meeting. [22.] You – sales managers and executives – might have trouble keeping your regular meetings productive. According to a survey we conducted last month, a fair percentage of the respondents feel their Monday morning meetings are an annoyance. [23.] The survey indicates some possible solutions. Before I give you the survey results, I'd like to remind you of today's schedule. After the morning talk, we'll have a lunch break. [24.] I regret to say that the cafeteria has limited seating. You could also buy lunch at one of the local delis. There are three within a minute's walk. After lunch, we will have a panel discussion with the renowned author, Alan Chung.

Questions

22. Who are the listeners?
   A. Business owners
   B. Consultants
   C. Managing staff
   D. Authors

23. What is the theme of the talk?
   A. How to make consulting successful
   B. How to have an effective meeting
   C. How to deal with part-time employees
   D. How to avoid annoyances during lunch

24. What does the speaker say about lunch?
   A. It is after the panel discussion.
   B. Not everyone can eat at the facility in the venue.
   C. Lunch sold in delis needs a few minutes to prepare.
   D. The participants will eat lunch with Alan Chung.

訳

皆さん、こんにちは。私は ACE Consulting の Ed Nielsen です。^{23.}今日はうまくいく会議についてお話します。^{22.}営業部長や経営幹部であるみなさんは生産性の高い会議をおこなうために苦労しているかも知れません。我々が先月おこなった調査によると、かなりの割合の回答者が月曜日の朝の会議がいらだたしいと感じています。^{23.}この調査はいくつかの解決法を示唆しています。調査の結果をお伝えする前に今日のスケジュールを確認しておきます。午前のトークのあとランチタイムです。^{24.}申し訳ありませんが館内レストランの席数は限られています。近くの弁当屋さんでランチを買うこともできます。歩いて1分の場所に3店舗あります。昼食後著名な著作者である Alan Chung さんをお迎えしてパネルディスカッションをおこないます。

Questions

22. 聞き手はだれですか？
    A. 経営者
    B. コンサルタント
    C. 経営スタッフ
    D. 著作者

23. トークのテーマは何ですか？
    A. コンサルティングを成功させる方法。
    B. 効果的な会議をする方法。
    C. パート従業員とのつきあい方。
    D. 昼食中のいらだちの回避法。

24. 話し手はランチに関して何を言っていますか？
    A. ランチはパネル・ディスカッションの後である。
    B. 全員が会場の施設で食べられる訳ではない。
    C. 弁当屋で売っているランチは準備に数分間必要だ。

D. 参加者は Alan Chung とランチを食べる。

ボキャブラリー a fair percentage かなりの割合　annoyance いらだち　I regret to say that〜 残念ながら〜です　deli 出来合いの総菜などを売っている店　renowned 著名な

参照 p. 34、p. 38

Questions 25-27（放送）

解答　25. B　26. A　27. B

スクリプト

[25.] Thanks for listening to *Life in Japan*. Today's topic is "Buying a house in Japan." If you are planning on working full-time or having a family in Japan, housing might be your first priority. Rent in Japan is among the highest in the world. You might prefer to buy and build up equity each month as you make mortgage payments instead of throwing away your money on rent. Now, let's get down to business. [26.] In Japan, tract housing is the mainstream. Tract housing is called "cookie-cutter housing" in North America. A plot of land is divided into several smaller lots. A small house is built on each lot. They look similar because, in most cases, building supplies are bought in bulk, which contributes to cutting down on the building cost. If you are thinking about living in the downtown Tokyo area, buying even a small tract house requires tons of elbow grease. However, you could find lots of real estate bargains in more rural areas. Now, get started looking for your dream house in Japan. [27.] We will be talking about how to take out a bank loan next time.

Questions

25. Who is the speaker?

　　A. A TV news anchor

B. A radio broadcaster

C. A magazine reporter

D. A real estate agent

26. Why does the speaker say, "Now, let's get down to business"?

A. To begin to talk about housing in Japan

B. To explain "cookie-cutter housing" in North America

C. To compare "cookie-cutter housing" with Japanese housing style

D. To warn them not to buy a house in downtown Tokyo

27. What is most likely the topic of the coming talk?

A. Getting a position at a Japanese bank

B. Dealing with financial institutions

C. Taking out a loan from real estate agents

D. Applying grease on one's elbows

訳

25. Life in Japan をお聞きいただきありがとうございます。今日のトピックは「日本で家を買う」です。もしあなたが日本で正社員になるとか家族を持つ予定なら、住宅が最重要になるでしょう。日本の家賃は世界で一番高い部類に入ります。毎月家賃を捨てるかわりに住宅ローンを支払うことで資産形成をしたほうがよいかもしれません。さあ、本論に入りましょう。26. 日本ではトラクト・ハウジング（建売住宅）が主流です。トラクト・ハウジングは北米では "cookie cutter housing" と呼ばれます。ひと続きの土地がいくつかの小さな区画に分けられます。小さな家が各区画に建てられます。どれも同じ家に見えます。それは、ほとんどの場合、建築資材が大量買いされるからです。それによって建築費をカットできます。もし東京の中心地で家を買おうと考えているなら、小さな家でもかなりの汗水を流さないといけないでしょう。

しかし、田舎ではかなりお買い得な不動産を見つけられます。さあ、日本であなたの夢の家を探し始めましょう。27. 次回は銀行ローンの引き出し方をお話しします。

25. 話し手は誰ですか？
   A. テレビのニュース司会者
   B. ラジオキャスター
   C. 雑誌リポーター
   D. 不動産業者

26. なぜ話し手は、"Now, let's get down to business." と言っていますか？
   A. 日本の住宅について話し始めるため。
   B. 北米の "cookie cutter housing" について説明するため。
   C. "cookie cutter housing" を日本の住宅スタイルと比較するため。
   D. 東京の中心地で家を買わないように警告するため。

27. 次のトークの話題はどれが一番あり得ますか？
   A. 日本の銀行で職を得ること。
   B. 金融機関と取引きすること。
   C. 不動産業者からローンを引き出すこと。
   D. 肘に油を塗ること。

> **ボキャブラリー**　tract housing ひとつの土地を分割して同じような家を立てるアメリカやカナダの建売住宅　bargain お買い得

参照　p. 19、p. 30、p. 41、p. 61

Questions 28-30 （ミーティングからの抜粋）

解答　28. C　29. C　30. A

スクリプト

[28.]As you know, the demand for fish and other seafood is skyrocketing. However, fishery resources have been depleted. Though we have developed the marine product procurement network throughout the world, it is becoming harder and harder to meet our customer demand. I think we have to shift our main product from raw fish to processed products. The latter's shelf life is much longer than that of raw fish. This policy change may help us secure a stable supply. Please look at the handout in front of you. These are the sales results of our processed seafood products in this quarter. We conducted a survey about consumer preferences of canned seafood last month. [29.]In accordance with the results, I think we should promote the sales for the one selling the second most this quarter. [30.]I'd like you to research the market demand yourselves and give me your feedback to help me decide what product we should promote most.

Questions

28. What can be inferred about the seafood business from the talk?

　A. Some commercial fisheries use skyrockets to catch fish.

　B. Sales reps catch and sell fishery resources themselves to meet their customer demands.

　C. Consumers eat more seafood than before.

　D. Some fishing boats have the satellite network system.

29. Look at the handout. Which of the following does the speaker want to promote most?

Fish Item	Cod	Sardines	Salmon	Herring
Net sales (tns.)	100	130	320	290

A. Cod

B. Salmon

C. Herring

D. Sardines

30. What does the speaker want the listeners to do?

A. To give her their research results

B. To get feedback from consumers

C. To tell her their preference of seafood

D. To conduct a consumer survey

訳

28. 皆さんも知っているように、魚やその他のシーフードの需要は急激に伸びています。しかし、漁業資源は枯渇しています。我々は世界中で海産物の調達ネットワークを作り上げてきましたが、顧客の需要を満たすことはより困難になっています。私は、我々の主力商品を鮮魚から加工品に移すべきだと考えます。後者の日持ちは鮮魚よりかなり長いです。この政策変更で安定供給を確保できる可能性があります。皆さんの前にあるハンドアウトを見てください。今四半期の加工海産物の売り上げ結果です。先月、缶詰シーフードに対する消費者の好みに関する調査をおこないました。29. その結果から、この四半期で2番目に売れた商品の販促をするべきであると私は考えます。30. どの商品を一番宣伝すべきかを決める助けになるよう、市場の需要を皆さん自身が調査し、フィードバックしてください。

28. このトークから、シーフード・ビジネスに関して何が推測できますか？

A. 商業漁業者には魚を捕まえるためにロケット花火を使う者もいる。

B. 営業社員は、顧客の需要を満たすため自分で漁業資源を捕獲し販売

する。

C. 消費者は以前よりもたくさんシーフードを食べる。

D. 衛星システムを持っている漁船がある。

29. ハンドアウトを見てください。話し手は次のどれを一番売りたいと思っていますか？

魚	タラ	イワシ	シャケ	ニシン
純売り上げ（tns.）	100	130	320	290

A. タラ

B. シャケ

C. ニシン

D. イワシ

30. 話し手は聞き手に何をしてほしいですか？

A. 調査結果を報告すること。

B. 消費者からフィードバックをもらうこと。

C. シーフードの好みを伝えること。

D. 消費者に調査をおこなうこと。

219

ボキャブラリー demand 需要　skyrocket（動）急上昇する、（名）ロケット花火、打ち上げ花火　procurement 調達、買い上げ、processed product 加工製品　secure a stable supply 安定供給を確保する　sales rep 営業社員　satellite network system 衛星ネットワーク

参照 p. 19、p. 34、p. 36、p. 60、p. 67、p. 95

あとがき

私の英語学習の始まりはリスニングとの出会いでした。形式重視の文法と訳文中心の英語授業で落ちこぼれだった私が、元通訳の先生に出会いました。その先生はネイティブスピーカー向けのラジオニュースをタイピングで打ち出してくるのです。ナチュラルな英語は当時の私には宇宙人の言葉のようでした。先生がタイピングした原稿を見ながら音声に合わせて読む練習をするのですが、初めはまったく歯が立ちません。

しかし、面白くて何回も練習するうちに少しついていけるようになりました。日本語とは違う英語独特の発音を自然に理解できたのでしょう。そして英語ニュースが少し聞こえてきた時の快感は今でも忘れられません。

この本の英語を速すぎると感じた方もいらっしゃると思いますが、ナチュラルな英語の音に慣れることは重要です。ビジネスや旅行で英語を使う時や、英検、TOEIC、TOEFL、IELTS などの英語試験を受ける時にはこの速さの英語を理解する必要があります。大学や大学院の入試でも高度なリスニング力が問われるようになってきています。

英語落ちこぼれだった私が最初からネイティブスピーカーの英語に触れられたことでリスニング強化できたように、くり返し練習することで必ずついていけるようになります。特に UNIT 1、UNIT 2 は繰り返し何回も練習することをおすすめします。リスニングは勉強というより練習です。努力は裏切りません。

最後に、この本を手に取っていただいた読者の方々に心からお礼申し上げます。皆さんの上達を心から願っています。

津村　元司

(著者紹介)

つむら　もとし
津村 元司

関西大学大学院外国語教育学研究科外国語分析領域前期博士課程修了（主席）。外国語
教育学修士。英検1級取得。
日米英語学院にて英検、TOEFL、IELTSなどの英語資格試験対策をはじめ、英語4技
能教育に長く携わる。
ヨーロッパ、アメリカやアジアでのインターナショナル・トレードショーにて樹脂製
品を出展し、プレゼンなどを多数回行いビジネス実務経験も豊富。韓国語も堪能。
[著書]『英語ライティングこれ一冊』（ベレ出版）

(執筆協力・英文校正)

Paul Aaloe （ポール・アロエ）

関西学院大学非常勤講師。カナダSimon Fraser大学でカナダ研究専攻。卒業後来日。
神戸YMCAランゲージセンター卒業。日本語能力検定1級取得。日本でEFL教育に長
年携わる。
教材開発にも数多く参加。フランス語、スウェーデン語も堪能。

収録音声　約3時間2分53秒
ナレーター　Guy Perryman　Howard Colefield　Jennifer Okano

- ── カバーデザイン　　糟谷 一穂
- ── DTP・本文図版　　株式会社 文昇堂

おんせい つき えいご いっさつ もんだい つよ てってい
[音声DL付] 英語リスニングこれ一冊 リスニング問題に強くなる徹底トレーニング

2021 年　4月25日　　初版発行

著者	つむら　もとし 津村 元司
発行者	内田 真介
発行・発売	ベレ出版 〒162-0832 東京都新宿区岩戸町12 レベッカビル TEL（03）5225-4790 FAX（03）5225-4795 ホームページ　https://www.beret.co.jp/
印刷	株式会社 文昇堂
製本	根本製本株式会社

ISBN978-4-86064-650-9 C2082　　　　　　　　　　編集担当　大石裕子